Business School

Managing operations

To be used with Unit 5

MBA Programme

The Open University, Walton Hall, Milton Keynes, MK7 6AA

First published 2011.

Edited, designed and typeset by The Open University

Printed in the United Kingdom by Hobbs the Printers Limited, Brunel Road, Totton, Hampshire SO40 3WX

ISBN 978 1780 0 7392 7

3.1

Contents

Introduction to *Managing operations*

Every manager faces organisational situations that can be better dealt with by **operations management** practices. These techniques tackle a number of organisational problems, ranging from the execution of simple tasks to the implementation of more complex processes involving several departments and people. An understanding of the principles of operations management is therefore important for all managers, because it provides a pragmatic way of looking at an organisation's processes. The need to manage manufacturing and service operations efficiently and effectively has led to a considerable increase in interest in operations management. In fact, the majority of most organisations' financial and human resources are invested in the activities involved in making products or delivering services.

Operations management is therefore critical to an organisation's success, and is one of the most important, challenging and exciting areas of business management. Operations management is:

- *important* because it is crucial to the competitiveness, sustainability and success of all types of organisations

- *challenging* because the ever-changing nature and dynamics of the business environment require organisations to continually adapt their operations to new requirements, demands, situations and expectations in the market

- *exciting* because, in order to make operations really contribute to the competitiveness and success of an organisation, operations managers need to be constantly active, creative and innovative in how they improve the company's operations.

Not surprisingly, there are many opportunities in the market for managers who want to engage with operations management activities. Although professionals working in this area do not always have 'Operations Manager' as their job title, they are invariably managing core activities within their companies. But what exactly is an operations manager? What do operations managers do? What sort of challenges and difficulties do they face? How do they deal with them? What kind of resources do they use? Who do they have to interact or negotiate with within and outside their organisation? When you have finished this book, you will be able to answer these and other important questions related to the area of operations.

This book will take you on a brief journey through the operations world. Your journey will start with a characterisation of 'operations' from a business perspective, where you will be able to develop your understanding of the **operations function**, its strategic importance for organisations in general and the main roles and responsibilities of managers involved with operations, whether they are called operations managers or not. You will then be introduced to core operations management practices that are regularly adopted by organisations around the world. Finally, your journey will end with a visit to the main managerial approaches applied to improve the performance of operations and some of the most contemporary issues challenging organisations in our globalised world.

Managing operations is divided into three main parts:

- Chapter 1, 'Understanding operations', introduces the operations function and describes the role of managers involved with operations activities. It also introduces the systemic perspective of operations and addresses strategic aspects of the area.

- Chapter 2, 'Managing operations', addresses relevant managerial theories, approaches and tools that are usually adopted in operations management practice.

- Chapter 3, 'Improving operations', focuses on managerial philosophies, approaches, concepts and models that can be applied to improve the quality and performance of operations. It also addresses important issues concerning the impact of the global business environment on an organisation's operations.

It is important to point out that the area of operations management involves a number of strategies, managerial approaches, tools, techniques and practices that will not be covered in this book. A more comprehensive study of the discipline would require far more time than the amount of hours you will dedicate to studying the contents of this book. However, the topics covered here represent fundamental approaches and practices that are relevant to most types of operations. Studying the book productively will give you a sound basis in the area, which will allow you to have a good understanding of operations in general as well as to deal better with operations issues in organisations you work for.

1: Understanding operations

This chapter introduces operations management, the role and purpose of the operations function, and the role of operations managers or managers involved with operations activities in their organisations. It will emphasise the strategic importance of the operations function, showing how it is central to the competitiveness and overall performance of organisations, whether they are small or large, for-profit or not-for-profit, manufacturing or service, private or public organisations. By studying this chapter you will also be able to understand the systemic dimension of operations, which facilitates the understanding of its main functionality and boundaries. Finally, you will be able to recognise that effective management of operations is crucial to reducing costs and adding value for customers.

1.1: Understanding operations management and the operations function

All organisations exist for a purpose. In practice, they all produce specific goods and/or specific services that represent the core products they deliver to their customers. Every day, we use a multitude of physical objects and a variety of services that have been manufactured or provided by organisations. Just as fish are said to be unaware of the water that surrounds them, most of us give little thought to the organisational activities that produce these goods and services we use. In simple terms, the study of operations management deals with how the goods and services that we buy and consume every day are produced.

Operations management is at the heart of most organisations. Whether the organisation is private or public, for-profit or not-for-profit, manufacturing or service, small or large, it needs to carry out its productivity activities efficiently and effectively. This is fundamental to maintaining and improving the prosperity and growth of the organisation.

After studying this section, you should be able to:

- define operations management and the role of operations managers
- understand the systemic perspective of operations
- identify and describe the main elements of a transformation system
- apply the transformation model to represent the operational system of an organisation.

Operations and operations management

Stop and reflect

Think about the meaning of operations. How would you define operations? What is involved in the management of operations?

In a broad sense, 'operation' is the action of making or producing something. This includes the way in which different elements or parts of a productive system work together. The 'management' of operations includes the design, implementation and improvement of the systems that produce an organisation's goods and/or services. These productive systems comprise the resources necessary for the production of goods or delivery of services required by customers. Typically, the resources in a productive system are materials, technologies, information and people.

Operations management is concerned with bringing these resources together and combining them to execute specific tasks of the **processes** that will produce and deliver the primary products (goods and/or services) of an organisation. These processes are linked chains of tasks or activities necessary to fulfil customer requests and they usually cut across different departments and functional units of an organisation. Working effectively with other functional units is one of the most important responsibilities of operations management.

It is important to realise that the aspects mentioned above address two essential concepts in operations management.

- 'Operations' refers to a productive system or, more specifically, to the operations function of organisations. This comprises the resources and processes that are arranged for the production and delivery of goods and services to the customers.

- 'Operations management' refers to a managerial activity and comprises the activities, decisions and responsibilities of designing, managing and improving the production and delivery of goods and services.

The following sub-section will help you develop a more comprehensive understanding of the operations function and the role of managers involved in operations management activities.

The role of the operations function and operations managers

Stop and reflect

In general terms, what is the main objective of the operations function of organisations?

A significant proportion of an organisation's resources, such as people, equipment, investments, installations, etc., is allocated to the operations function. As customers or users of many products from a number of different companies, it is not difficult to gain at least a partial view of the operations of the organisations we visit in our day-to-day life. One practical way of gaining initial insights into the operations function of a company is to identify the end product (goods or service) that the company delivers. Once this is clear, the identification of the resources – people, equipment, facilities, etc. – the company employs to produce and deliver its main product gives additional insights into its operations.

Every organisation has an operations function. However, it is important to bear in mind that not all organisations call their operations function by this name. Within large and complex organisations operations is usually a major functional area, with people specifically designated to take responsibility for managing all or part of the organisation's operations processes. It is an important functional area because it plays a crucial role in determining how well an organisation satisfies its customers. In the case of private sector companies, the overall performance of the operations function is usually expressed in terms of profits, growth and competitiveness; in public and voluntary organisations, it is often expressed in terms of providing value for money for **stakeholders** – for example, taxpayers or donors want to know that the money they provide is being used sensibly.

Understanding the principles of operations management is important for all managers, because the principles provide a systemic way of looking at an organisation's productive processes. The need to manage manufacturing and service operations efficiently and effectively has led to a considerable increase of interest in operations management in recent years.

Creating value for customers

Because customers are vital to the survival of most organisations, and customers usually want value for their money, it is fundamentally important for operations managers to understand how operations activities can add value to the products (goods and services) delivered to customers. In general, there are two types of activities that can influence the productivity of organisations: value-adding activities, which are the activities that add value to the end product, and non-value-adding activities, which are the activities that waste resources and fail to add value to the end product.

Typically, operations take in various inputs that pass through several processes that add value to those inputs. The 'value' added refers to all features and specifications added to the goods or services that the customers are willing to pay for. Operations can improve the performance and competitive advantage of organisations by focusing on developing the value-adding activities and eliminating the non-value-adding ones.

The value chain model (Porter, 1985) depicts key activities that organisations can develop or manage with the purpose of adding value for customers. The model describes different value-adding activities that connect an organisation's supply side with its demand side (Figure 1.1). As we can see in Figure 1.1, 'operations', including **logistics** activities, are seen by Porter as one of the primary activities of organisations. The primary activities are core activities that contribute directly to the production and delivery of goods and services to customers. The support activities, which are as important as the core ones, enable or facilitate the execution of the primary activities; for example, the human resource function is a support function responsible for recruiting and developing people who might have crucial roles within the operations function. It is hard to think of an operation that does not require people; even the most automated operations need people to monitor the machinery or technological devices being used in the process.

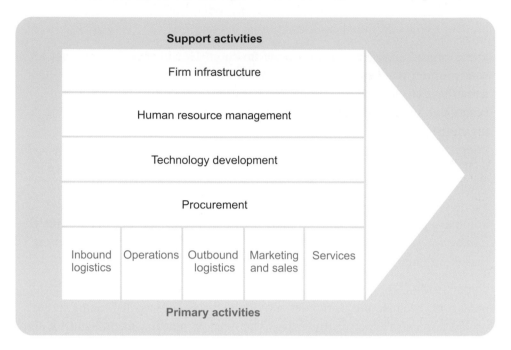

Figure 1.1: The value chain model
(Source: Porter, 1985)

Defining the operations manager role

Stop and reflect

What do operations managers do? Are there managers in your organisation carrying out activities similar to the ones that operations managers generally do?

Usually organisations have managers who are responsible for managing some or all of the resources required by the operations function. These managers are commonly called **operations managers**, but organisations may use different names or terms – for example, a freight provider might call its operations manager 'freight manager'. Regardless of their title, managers involved with the operations function are responsible for managing core production resources and activities of an organisation. This includes sourcing goods and/or services from suppliers, designing and monitoring transformation processes and managing the delivery of products to customers.

Some people argue that operations management involves everything an organisation does. In this sense, every manager is an operations manager, since all managers are ultimately responsible for contributing to the activities required to create and deliver an organisation's goods or services. However, others argue that this definition is too wide, and that the operations function is about producing the right amount of goods or services, at the right time, of the right quality and at the right cost to meet customer requirements.

A consensual position would be that operations managers are responsible for managing activities that are directly involved in the production of goods and services. Their responsibilities include design and development of operations processes, planning and control, performance improvement, and so forth (these and other operations aspects will be discussed later on). In their day-to-day activities, they have to interact with managers from other functional areas that are affected by, or have an impact on, the operations function. Such areas include marketing, finance, accounting, human resources and engineering.

Decision making is a central role of all operations managers. They have to make decisions about what technology to adopt or replace, the resources and staff necessary for the operations, adequate operations capacity to face predicted – and sometimes unpredicted – demand, adequate suppliers for the operations, the proper systems and tools to help operations planning and control, the best performance level for the operations, and so forth. The five main kinds of decisions that operations managers usually make relate to the:

- processes by which goods and services are produced
- quality of goods or services
- quantity of goods or services (the **capacity** of operations)
- stock of materials (**inventory**) needed to produce goods or services
- management of human resources involved with operations activities.

In addition, operations managers have to make sure that the operations meet customers' requirements, health and safety standards, and high levels of quality and dependability. They also have to make the operations flexible enough to respond quickly to new requirements and demands. Operations management is an exercise in constant improvement and everything must be done in the most efficient and cost-effective way.

There are several managerial approaches that help operations managers deal with the challenges and difficulties they face: the operations management discipline has significantly evolved over the years and nowadays many managerial practices for planning, controlling, designing and improving operations are well established and generally applicable to different organisational contexts. Capacity management strategies, process technologies, quality control approaches and 'lean' management practices are among the main operations management aspects you will read about later on in this book.

When developing their managerial activities, operations managers usually deal with many people inside and outside the organisation. Internally, many operations processes flow both from and to other organisational functions, such as marketing, human resources, finance, etc. Good communication between operations and other functional areas is therefore essential, as operations managers have to be able to explain their own plans to other functions. They also have to make clear the operational implications of what other functions are trying to achieve. Externally, operations managers have to deal, directly or indirectly, with suppliers and customers. Therefore, developing good relationships with these groups is essential.

The transformation model of operations

The discussion above has highlighted the role of operations in creating and delivering the goods or services produced by an organisation for its customers. In this sub-section, we introduce the **transformation model** for analysing operations. This is shown in Figure 1.2, which represents the main elements of an operations system: inputs, transformation processes, outputs and feedback.

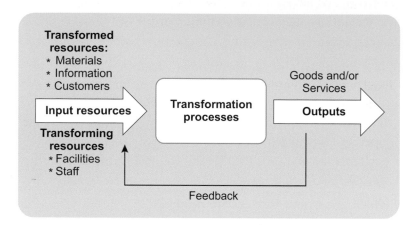

Figure 1.2: The transformation model of operations
(Source: adapted from Galloway et al., 2000, p. 35)

From a system perspective, business operations can be seen as a productive system whose processes *transform* specific resources (*inputs*) into finished goods or services (*outputs*) required by customers. This basic transformation model applies equally in manufacturing and service organisations, and in both the private and the not-for-profit sectors.

The input–transformation–output model is a useful way of thinking about how resources are transformed into goods or services (Figure 1.2). In general, any process in which inputs are transformed into outputs can be seen as an 'operation'. Next, we are going to look at each of the elements in Figure 1.2 in more detail.

Inputs

Typically, the input resources might include materials, equipment, energy, capital, information and people. Some of the input resources are themselves transformed in the process to form part of the output. These are called **transformed resources** (Slack et al., 2007) and they are usually a mixture of:

- Materials – some operations transform the physical properties of materials, such as clay for brick-making or food in a restaurant. Other operations transform the location of materials, as in the case of parcels and mail in the postal services. Others transform the possession of the materials, such as retail operations; and yet others, such as warehouses, just store materials.

- Information – some operations transform the form of the information (e.g., consultants, accountants), others sell information (e.g., market research companies), others transport information (e.g., telecommunications companies) and others store information (e.g., libraries).
- Customers – some operations transform customers physically (e.g., hairdressing, hospitals, dentists), some transform the psychological state of customers (e.g., entertainment companies), some transport customers (e.g., airline companies) and others accommodate customers (e.g., hotels).

Another set of inputs to any operation is called **transforming resources**. These are the resources necessary to act upon the transformed resources to carry out the transformation, but they do not themselves form part of the output. These can be:

- Facilities or fixed assets – the buildings, machinery, plant and process technologies of the operation.
- Staff – the people involved in the operation, at any level. They are usually referred to as human resources and they are the employees of the organisation carrying out the operations. These are the people who plan, control, operate or maintain the operation. The nature of the staff differs between operations. For example, a factory assembling toys may not need staff with a very high level of technical skills. In contrast, a consultancy firm depends largely on staff highly skilled in their particular area. In this situation, the level of human resources' skills and knowledge is crucial for the quality of the operation.

The staff involved in the transformation processes may include both people who are directly employed by the organisation and those contracted to supply services to it. They are sometimes described as 'labour'. The facilities of an organisation – including buildings, machinery and equipment – are sometimes referred to as 'capital'. Operations vary greatly in the mix of labour and capital that make up their inputs. Highly automated operations depend largely on capital; others rely mainly on labour.

Transformation processes

The transformation processes comprise the group of activities that takes one or more inputs, transforms the inputs, adding value to them, and provides the outputs to the customers. The transformation processes may include:

- changes in the physical characteristics of materials or customers (e.g., food processing, a hair cut)
- changes in the location of materials, information or customers (e.g., cargo freight, telecommunications, public transport)
- changes in the ownership of materials or information (e.g., retail, market data)
- storage or accommodation of materials, information or customers (e.g., warehousing, information backup storage, a bed and breakfast hotel)
- changes in the purpose or form of information (e.g., information processing)

- changes in the physiological or psychological state of customers (e.g., a spa hotel).

Where the inputs are raw materials, it is relatively easy to identify the transformation involved, as when milk is transformed into cheese and butter. Where the inputs are information or people, the nature of the transformation may be less obvious. For example, a hospital aims to transform ill patients (the input) into healthy patients (the output).

Often, all three types of transformed inputs – materials, information and customers – are transformed by the same organisation. For example, withdrawing money from a bank involves staff updating information about the customer's account and then providing the customer with cash. Treating a patient in a hospital involves the staff assessing the patient's state of health and then providing treatment to the patient.

Several different transformations are usually required to produce goods or services.

Outputs

The outputs from transformation processes are usually goods and services. While goods are essentially tangible, services are intangible by nature. Goods are physical products of the process; they are typically produced prior to the customer receiving them. On the other hand, we cannot touch or store a service. Services are consumed at the time of production.

Many operations produce both goods and services. For example, a consultancy firm provides services that may also produce printed (physical) reports as outputs. A restaurant typically provides a service that includes the production of goods (food) as outputs.

Finally, undesirable outputs may result from the transformation process. These are usually the waste elements generated in the production process. Relevant issues concerning the operations management of undesirable outputs include:

- minimising the environmental impact caused by waste outputs
- preserving the health and safety of employees and local community.

In addition, the operations function may be responsible for ethical behaviour in relation to the social impact of transformation processes, both locally and globally. For example, in the US, manufacturers of sports footwear have come under fire for employing child labour and paying low wages to workers employed in their overseas factories.

Feedback

Feedback information is used to control the operations system by adjusting the inputs and transformation processes that are used to achieve desired outputs. For example, a chef relies on a flow of information from the customer, through the waiter, about the quality of the food. Adverse feedback might lead the chef to change the inputs (e.g., by buying better-quality potatoes) or the transformation process (such as changing the recipe or the cooking method).

Feedback is essential for operations managers. It can come from both internal sources (which may include performance monitoring and quality control staff and systems) or external sources (which may include individual customers and/or organisations served by the operations).

1.2: Strategic dimension and objectives of operations

The majority of most organisations' human, technological and financial resources are invested in the activities involved in making products or delivering services to customers. A significant proportion of these resources is allocated to the operations function, which plays a crucial role in fulfilling the needs of customers. Operations management is therefore critical to organisational success; it can 'make or break' any organisation.

In this section, we will focus on strategic aspects of operations. It is the operations strategy that sets the general principles that will support decision-making processes and provides the basis for defining the operations role in an organisation.

After studying this section, you should be able to:

- justify the strategic importance of operations to organisations
- explain how operations management can add value for customers
- identify and describe key strategic performance objectives that apply to all types of organisations.

Operations strategy

Stop and reflect

Why is the operations function strategically important to organisations?

We have seen that the operations function comprises all the activities required to create and deliver goods and/or services to customers. This applies equally to both private and not-for-profit organisations. Operations strategy comprises the total pattern of decisions and actions that sets the role, objectives and activities of the operations function. It contributes to and supports the organisation's **business strategy**, providing the link between business strategy and operations decisions.

Operations strategy is constrained within the context of an organisation's corporate and business strategies. This hierarchy of strategy is shown in Figure 1.3. As the arrows show, although the main influence of strategy flows downward (top down) from corporate to business to functional strategy, there is also an influence in the reverse direction (bottom up), from functional to business and up to corporate strategy.

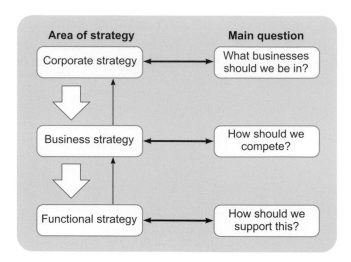

Figure 1.3: The strategy hierarchy

In a large, diversified organisation, any organisational unit must formulate and execute its strategy within the context of the strategies of the organisation as a whole. For example, an individual hotel that is part of a big chain of hotels, such as Hilton or Accor, must be managed within the overall strategy established by the corporation to which it belongs.

The four-stage model

For manufacturing businesses, Hayes and Wheelwright (1984) have provided a classification of the ways in which the operations function contributes to the overall competitiveness of the organisation. This framework, shown in Figure 1.4, has subsequently been extended to service organisations by Chase and Hayes (1991). It is called the 'four-stage model' because it suggests that the operations function moves through four stages of contributing to competitiveness.

	Neutral	Supportive
Internally	*Stage I* *Internally neutral* Objective is to minimise the negative impact of 'operations'	*Stage III* *Internally supportive* Objective is for 'operations' to provide credible support for the business strategy
Externally	*Stage II* *Externally neutral* Objective is for 'operations' to help the business maintain parity with its competitors	*Stage IV* *Externally supportive* Objective is for 'operations' to provide a source of competitive advantage

Figure 1.4: The four-stage model of the operations function's contribution to organisational competitiveness
(Source: based on Neely, 1998)

Table 1.1 presents a further characterisation of the four stages in the model.

Table 1.1: Characteristics of the four-stage model of the operations function

Stage	Description	Objective	Operations function's performance	What it means for organisations
I	Internally neutral	To minimise the negative impact of 'operations'	Not as well as the other functional areas, which may have to make up for its shortfall	May be unaware that they are not competitive, either not realising that operations can provide a competitive advantage or not appreciating how the operations function in other organisations is performing
II	Externally neutral	For 'operations' to help the business maintain parity with its competitors	At least as well as the other functional areas, but does not provide any competitive edge	May be aware that operations does not provide a competitive advantage, but not yet starting to improve the operations function or have been unsuccessful in improving it
III	Internally supportive	For 'operations' to provide credible support for the business strategy	Provides a competitive edge, performing as well as the best organisations in its sector	Aware of the role of the operations function in contributing to strategic advantage, but not yet exploiting it as a source of persistent competitive advantage
IV	Externally supportive	For 'operations' to provide a source of competitive advantage	Source of persistent competitive advantage	The operations function may be described as 'world-class', providing a competitive advantage in the organisation's current activities and a basis for future activities in new areas

Strategic performance objectives

In a market characterised by increased competition and high customer expectations, the overall performance of the operations function is crucial for the success of any organisation. Performing well is a business imperative. Successful organisations maintain their reputation largely due to the performance of their operations. Every organisation wants to be efficient and effective: the main objective of operations management is to arrange a company's productivity resources and activities in as effective and efficient a way as possible. 'Being effective' means producing the goods and services that customers really want; 'being efficient' means producing them with as little effort or cost as possible.

Stop and reflect

How do organisations know whether or not their operations are performing well?

In order to know whether its operations function is succeeding, a company needs to determine specific performance objectives against which its success can be measured. Typically, these performance objectives are critical success factors that are strategically important to the organisation as a whole. Being strategically important means that the performance objectives have to be considered as strategic goals to be achieved and the operations function must develop the appropriate operations resources to support the achievement of these goals. Usually, the operations performance objectives are specifically related to satisfying customers' requirements.

The five key strategic performance objectives of operations

Operations resources must be selected, deployed and managed with the purpose of creating the goods and services that will contribute to the achievement of an organisation's business strategy. In this sense, we can say that the contribution made by an operations function is crucial for the long-term success of an organisation. Generally, there are five strategic performance objectives that the operations function is expected to support (Figure 1.5).

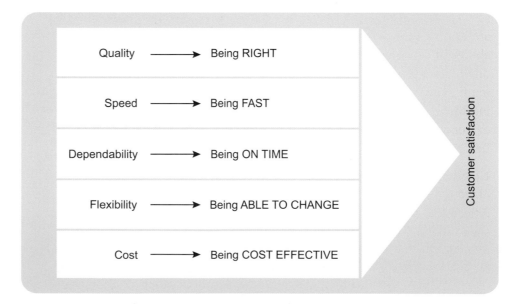

Figure 1.5: The five key strategic performance objectives (Source: adapted from Slack et al., 2007)

Quality – quality is about doing things right. It means consistently producing goods and services that meet customers' expectations. The quality objective can be achieved by the provision of error-free products that fulfil customer requirements. This requires a skilled workforce, adequate job specifications, proper technologies and effective communication. For example, the quality of a bus company can mean that staff are courteous and helpful, the drivers drive safely, the buses are clean and quiet and the timetable is easy to read.

Speed – doing things quickly. It is about delivering goods and services to customers as fast as possible. This involves making quick decisions and rapidly moving materials and information inside the operations. For example, broadcasting companies typically want to be the first to broadcast breaking news. Speed is also essential for emergency services, where the fast delivery of a service can be a matter of life or death.

Dependability – doing things on time and keeping the delivery promises made to customers. It is about developing trustworthiness. Dependability can be achieved through the use of reliable equipment, effective communication, efficient scheduling systems, a motivated workforce, etc. For example, in a supermarket dependability could mean keeping to reasonable queuing times, constant availability of parking, keeping the proportion of goods out of stock to a minimum, etc.

Flexibility – being able to change the operation to fulfil new customer requirements. As different customers have different requirements and these requirements can change over time, organisations need to develop their operations ability to introduce new or modified goods and services (*good/ service flexibility*), as well as to produce a wide range or mix of goods and services (*mix flexibility*). Flexibility also involves *volume flexibility* – the ability to change volume of output over time – and *delivery flexibility* – the ability to change delivery time. Flexibility can be achieved by the use of more versatile equipment, suppliers with good flexibility performance, a multi-skilled workforce, etc. For example, a retailer with the ability to introduce new goods or promotions and the ability to provide a wide range of goods is performing well in terms of both good/service flexibility and mix flexibility.

Cost – doing things economically. Low cost is a universally attractive objective (Slack et al., 2007). Lower cost of producing goods and services is reflected to the customer in the form of lower price. Usually, operations spend money on staff, materials, facilities, equipment and technology. Cost reduction can be achieved by developing good relationships with suppliers, by good negotiation of supplying contracts, by getting the right mix of resources and facilities as inputs, etc. The example overleaf describes how a retailer manages to keep its operational costs to a minimum level.

Aldi: keeping down costs

Aldi is an international supermarket specialising in 'private-label', mainly food products. It has carefully focused its services concept and delivery system to attract customers in a highly competitive market. The company believes its unique approach to operations makes it 'virtually impossible' for competitors to match its combination of price and quality.

Aldi operations are deliberately simple, using basic facilities to keep down overhead costs. Most stores stock only a limited range of goods. The 'private-label' approach means that the products have been produced according to Aldi's quality specifications and are sold only in Aldi stores. Without the high costs of brand marketing and advertising, and with Aldi's formidable purchasing power, prices can be 30 per cent below their branded equivalents.

Other cost-saving practices include open-carton displays, which eliminate the need for special shelving, no provision of grocery bags (this saves costs by encouraging customers to reuse their own bags and is also environmentally friendly!) and using a 'trolley rental' system, which requires customers to return the trolley to the store to get their coin deposit back.

(Source: adapted from Slack et al., 2007, p. 50)

Conclusion to chapter 1

This chapter has introduced some fundamental concepts and perspectives of the discipline of operations management. At this stage, you should be aware that organisations can be seen as operations that generate and offer specific outputs (goods and/or services) to a market. The outputs are generated through specific transformation processes that are designed to add some sort of value to the specific inputs taken from the environment until the final products (goods and/or services) are ready. The inputs are the resources that will be transformed into final products as well as the resources that will help with the transformation processes. This systemic perspective of the operations is well illustrated by the transformation model of operations, which is a graphical representation of the main elements of operations systems in general (inputs–transformation–outputs–feedback).

Operations management is therefore the management of the operations function (an essential part of all organisations) and involves many important activities, such as planning, design, implementation, control and improvement of the activities and resources necessary to produce the organisation's goods and/or services.

The main objective of the operations function is to arrange the resources necessary for the production and delivery of goods and/or services. It is where the core activities of the transformation process occur. Not uncommonly, in many organisations the operations function is not a 'visible' department or area of the organisation. The core operations activities are performed by people working in several departments of the organisation; managers of the operations function (not necessarily called 'operations managers') manage essential parts of core operations activities, such as:

- managing production resources
- sourcing goods and/or services from suppliers
- designing and monitoring production processes
- managing the delivery of products to customers.

These core activities add value to customers by adding specific features and specifications to inputs that will be transformed into a final good or service that the customers will pay for. Typically, in the manufacturing sector, the customers see the final product after the transformation processes are performed; whereas in the service sector, the customers usually see the transformation processes during the delivery of the service.

Finally, it is important to bear in mind that organisations usually allocate a significant proportion of human, technological and financial resources to the operations function, which plays a crucial role in fulfilling the customers' needs. This is why the operations function is strategically important to all organisations.

2: Managing operations

This chapter introduces you to some of the key managerial theories, approaches and techniques that are commonly adopted in operations management practice. By studying this chapter you will learn some of the main concepts, tools and techniques that support managers and their organisations to design, plan and control operations. You will also learn about the main categories of process technologies and their impact on the operations function. Finally, you will be introduced to some important aspects of logistics and supply chain management and their impact on costs and value creation.

2.1: Operations design

All operations managers are designers, but in a much broader sense than just designing the look of a product. Although operations managers do not necessarily have direct responsibility for the design of a product, they usually play an important role in providing the information and advice on which the successful development of the product depends. Typically, operations managers are more involved with the design of the processes that will produce the goods and services to be delivered to customers.

This section will focus on fundamental aspects of 'process' design, which is concerned with the physical arrangements of the facilities, technologies, people and activities that produce the goods and services delivered by an organisation.

After studying this section, you should be able to:

- characterise generic process types according to the different combinations of volume and variety
- compare and contrast different process types in manufacturing and service operations
- discuss the implications of layout and flow design on operations performance.

Process design

When studying Chapter 1 you saw that the manufacturing of goods and delivery of services require certain processes to be executed. It is also necessary to allocate adequate and appropriate resources that will facilitate and support the execution of these processes. Finally, the activities or tasks within processes need to be completed in a determined order or sequence that allows each task to add something to the whole process of production or delivery.

It is important to bear in mind that 'tasks' and 'processes' are not the same thing. Essentially, the difference between a 'task' and a 'process' is similar to the difference between a 'part' and the 'whole'. A task is a unit of work, an activity normally performed by one person; a process comprises a group of tasks that together give a specific value to the product or delivery method that adds to the final value offered to the customer (Hammer, 1996).

Process types

Considering the most appropriate design for an operations process centres on two key questions:

How much will the process need to produce? The *volume* of the output can range from very few – even a single output (e.g., a new bridge or ship from a construction project) to very many, in the case of **standardised** mass-produced consumer goods such as motor cars or take-away hamburgers.

To what extent will the outputs of the process be alike and to what extent will they differ from each other? The *variety* of the output will also range from very low – where each unit of output of goods or service is exactly like every other unit of output, as in the case of consumer goods such as sugar or the food in fast-food restaurants – to very high, as in the case of high-fashion clothing, consultations with medical specialists or the food in five-star restaurants.

Stop and reflect

How do volume and variety influence the design of a process?

Operations processes must be carefully designed to take into account both the current volume and variety required for goods or services and any likely future changes to that volume and variety. Typically, as the volume of outputs produced by an organisation increases, the level of variety tends to decrease. This relationship is so consistent that it is possible to identify five different combinations of volume and variety, which in operations we describe as the five generic process types. These five types are known as projects, jobbing, batch production, mass production and continuous production, as illustrated in Figure 2.1.

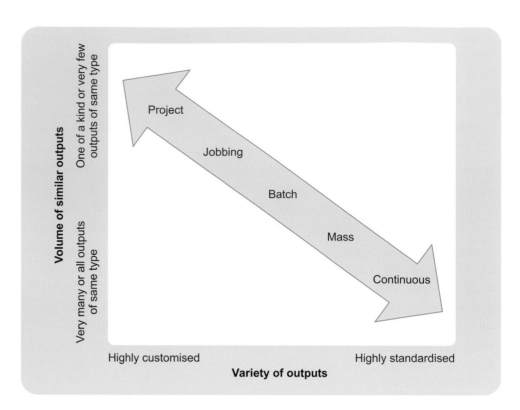

Figure 2.1: The five process types

Beginning from the upper left-hand corner of Figure 2.1, **project** is a type of operations that typically produce one finished output at a time to customer requirements. They generally take a long time to complete and involve large capital and labour investments relative to the size of the operation. For example, most types of construction and civil engineering, as well as the manufacture of large and complex products such as aeroplanes and ships are organised around projects. Projects are, by their nature, complex and uncertain, and run a high risk of failure or cost and time overruns. This is especially true of projects involving untried technologies or novel situations, such as large projects that require IT equipment and systems upgrading, or constructing and launching artificial space satellites.

While many activities are organised as projects, most productive systems are organised around processes in which activities are repeated rather than taking place only once. **Jobbing** operations are usually chosen for processes in which, although outputs vary, volume is higher than in project operations. Jobbing operations process many different jobs to specific customer requirements and work is intermittent rather than continuous. Each customer job is processed by the operation individually and may require many different work activities before work is complete. As an analogy, you might think about your visits to a supermarket or shopping centre. You probably follow a somewhat different route through the store from any other customer, and buy a different selection of goods, resulting in a unique and individual experience. A typical jobbing operation for producing goods would be a custom print shop; an example of a job would be designing and printing a letterhead for a personal or business customer.

When the volume of output is higher, and more outputs are identical, batch production may be the best choice of process type. In **batch** production, many different outputs are processed at the same time, in groups or batches.

This is the most common process type for repetitive operations, and you can probably think of many examples. A commercial bakery will probably use batch production for baking bread, for instance. Batch production systems usually operate at higher volumes than jobbing operations, and the outputs are often not produced for an individual customer. Batch production is applied in service as well as manufacturing contexts. For example, in schools, a class of students could be considered as being a batch that is being acted on by the teacher. An administrator sending out a standard letter to a large number of people might use the 'mail merge' function to insert each recipient's name and address (and sometimes other personal information) into each letter, rather than typing this onto each letter individually.

In **mass production processes**, large volumes of standardised products are made for a mass market. This process type is appropriate for markets that demand high volumes of a similar output. Mass-produced goods include cars, personal computers and many household products. Mass production processes often use ways of linking the different stages of the process, such as assembly lines, which are automated transfer systems that link different workstations and impose a standard pace. Similarly, the customer billing operations of an electricity supplier, where information is held in a large centralised customer database and printed out in bulk, can be considered a type of mass production.

Some highly standardised products are made using **continuous** production, where the system is highly automated, runs with only intermittent stops (often 24 hours a day, 365 days a year) and outputs are difficult to separate physically. Many continuous production systems are found in processing industries such as petrochemicals and foodstuffs.

Choosing a process type

Given these five choices of process type, how will an organisation find the best one for its outputs of goods or services? Look back at Figure 2.1 and you will notice that the five process types lie along a diagonal that ranges from low-volume/high-customisation to high-volume/high-standardisation. This is because the process type for any good or service must be consistent with the volume and variety of the output. The best process strategy is found on the diagonal; process strategies that are not on the diagonal generally have either over-invested in the process or provided too much/not enough flexibility to customise the product to market demands, as shown in Figure 2.2. As volume increases, for example, it becomes more difficult to customise outputs to individual customer requirements. For instance, you might expect a taxi (low volume of customers) to take you from door-to-door (high variety of delivery), but a bus (high volume of customers) will only take you from one bus stop to another (low variety of delivery).

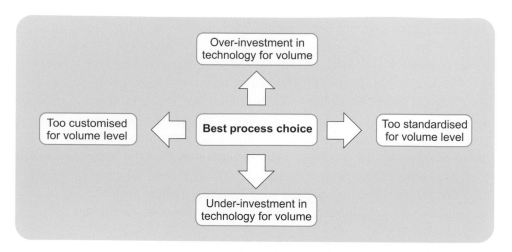

Figure 2.2: Implications of operating off the diagonal

While organisations tend to operate on the diagonal shown in Figure 2.1, it is possible for some innovative organisations to operate off it when they identify and move into market niches where a different process type is more appropriate for the dominant market. For example, some car companies have managed to operate in a sustainable niche in low-volume/low-variety car assembly. This is in contrast to the mainstream car market, where major assemblers try to achieve high volumes of more standardised products. Other innovators have tried to use the opportunities offered by advances in technology and new thinking about mass manufacturing to, in effect, move off the diagonal by achieving high variety with high volume. Such manufacturers may attempt 'mass customisation' (Pine, 1992) by offering a wide range of 'factory-standard' options. For example, the success of mass production computer manufacturers like Dell is largely based on their ability to provide 'build to order' machines.

It is important to bear in mind that the choice of process type will affect every aspect of the operation.

Service process types

When reading through the definitions of the five process types, you may have found it difficult to apply them to service organisations. Schmenner (1986) suggested that service operations might be more easily classified by the degree of customisation and the degree of labour intensity (instead of volume). Figure 2.3 shows his suggestions for classifying services into different process types: professional service, service shop, mass service and service factory.

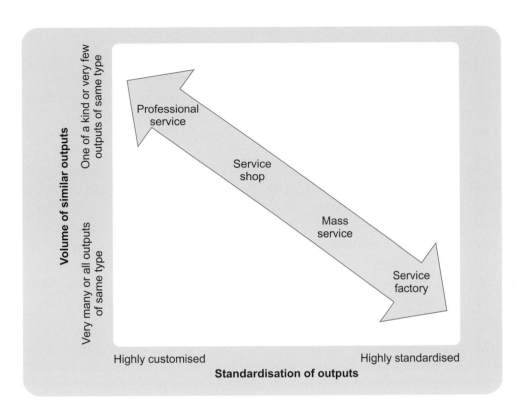

Figure 2.3: The four service process types

Professional services are usually provided by highly trained specialists, such as medical doctors or lawyers. Services are tailored to each client or customer and are very labour intensive.

Service shops are usually provided by trained specialists, but with less customisation and less labour intensity – good examples are universities and travel shops, where each individual is treated slightly differently but the range of services is much more standardised.

Mass services offer the same basic service to every customer, as with banks or supermarkets, and there is much less interaction with the service provider.

Service factories have very little customisation, as with the case of public transportation, and an individual client or customer has very little interaction with the service provider.

Western and Japanese approaches to process design

The objective of the design process is to reduce the risks associated with a new product, while still ensuring the earliest possible launch. The process involves a trade-off between risk reduction and the cost of delay. The greater the delay, the more likely it is that a competitor will launch their own product, thereby gaining the competitive advantage of being first to market. In some industries the 'time to market' – that is, the time from deciding to develop a concept to its market launch – is vital to commercial success. Failing to be the first to market, or at least a fast follower, generally decreases revenues and profits and increases the risk of failure – a 'me too' or repetitive product (with no differential features) has few competitive advantages. This is particularly true in markets with rapidly changing technology. Japanese companies of electrical consumer goods and motor cars are known for their ability to develop a constant stream of new models faster than their competitors. One reason for this is the way the companies have managed the design process using multifunctional teams.

The traditional Western approach to new product design and development has been likened to a relay race. Responsibility for the project passes from department to department in turn like a baton – from research and development people who design the product, to operations people who produce it, to sales who sell it. There are a number of problems with this sequential approach.

Each department concentrates on its own priorities without due regard for the legitimate concerns of the others, which can lead to:

- products being designed without regard to how they will be manufactured
- technological overkill, as designers seek perfectionist solutions without regard for cost or the performance required in the marketplace
- the practice of one department not starting work until the other finishes its work that lengthens the development time
- time lost in seeking solutions to problems originating from earlier stages in the process, requiring the project to be handed back. Further costs and delays invariably accumulate as people seek to place the blame on other departments.

The Japanese approach, in contrast, has been likened to a football team where the ball – the project – is interchanged between team members to make best use of their skills at the appropriate times. A project team is made up of players from research and development, operations and sales. Departmental barriers are removed and the players from the different departments can ensure that the others are aware of relevant issues (sales people ensuring a customer focus, operations ensuring manufacturability in design, etc.). When well managed, this concurrent approach – often termed 'simultaneous engineering' – offers faster and better new product design and development.

Stop and reflect

Think about your organisation or one you are familiar with. Can you recognise which type of process design is adopted by the company?

Layout and flow

Once a decision has been made about where the production process is to be positioned along the volume–variety diagonal, it is then possible to undertake a more detailed process design.

There are two main elements of the process to be designed: layout and flow. The term **layout** is usually used to describe the arrangement of physical facilities for producing goods and services, while **flow** describes how materials, information or customers move through the operations system.

Layout types

As Figure 2.4 shows, there are four basic layout types. Each has implications for the design of jobs of process operators, for the ability of the system to respond to changes in demand and for the level of inventory (in manufacturing systems more particularly).

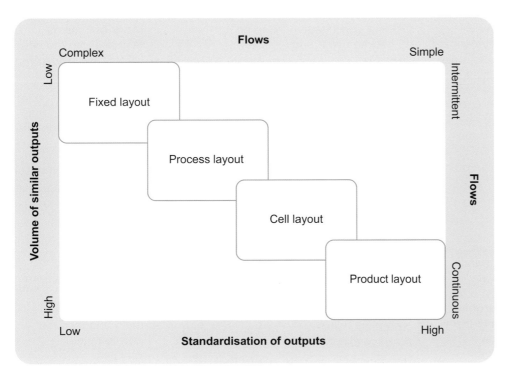

Figure 2.4: The four physical layout types

Table 2.1 provides a comparative description of the four physical layout types shown in Figure 2.4.

Table 2.1: Details of the four physical layout types

Layout type	Description	Advantages	Disadvantages	Examples
Fixed position	Operation takes place in one position, where all necessary resources are located, including staff and equipment Usually associated with projects	High flexibility High variety of tasks for staff Little disturbance for the product or customers	Likely to incur high unit costs Difficult to schedule Involves lots of movement of staff and equipment	Construction projects, e.g., motorways and bridges Large manufactured items, e.g., oil tankers and aeroplanes Entertainment, catering and other activities associated with special events, e.g., weddings, country fairs or music festivals
Process (functional) layout	Equipment and operators are arranged according to common processes; work travels between them	High flexibility Varied and hence more interesting work for operators Not easily disrupted	Often hard to control Associated with low utilisation and high work-in-progress (leading to high material stock costs in manufacturing and unhappy customers in services)	A school where students travel between classrooms, the library and other facilities
Cell layout	Resources (e.g., equipment and operators) for each particular type of product are grouped together in cells	Offers a good trade-off between cost and flexibility Can be used to achieve high throughput, as well as providing more interesting work for operators	Can be costly to initiate Needs higher investment in equipment Offers minimal inventory levels within its operations High stocks of the cell's raw materials and finished goods if its input and output aren't coordinated with other operations	Many automated factories use the cell layout, as do some cafeterias
Product layout	Equipment and operators are arranged in order of the stages of the process and the product travels between them	Offers lowest unit cost for high volume Facilitates the use of specialised equipment, with correspondingly specialist jobs designed to minimise movements	Not very flexible Very repetitive jobs; workers can be bored and frustrated In manufacturing, work-in-progress inventory is minimised, but needs a continuous supply of raw material (from a high level of input material or frequent deliveries from suppliers) or the line will quickly halt	A car assembly plant, where cars are progressively assembled from parts and modules into complete vehicles The arrivals facilities at airports, where you are sequenced from the gate to passport control to baggage claim with very few alternative routes available

Choosing appropriate layout

As you might expect, while there is some flexibility in choosing layout and flow for an operation, some patterns are more appropriate than others for particular process types. Decisions about layout and flow will affect performance through their impact on:

- cost and flexibility of the process
- time and distance that materials or customers travel in the process
- flow of materials, information and customers through the operation.

Process layout planning requires consideration as to how work flows vary between different activities. There are many numerical techniques, from simple to sophisticated, for comparing process layouts and trying to determine which would minimise distance travelled or the number of movements between different activities. Some of these techniques can be done with pencil and paper, by looking at which activities have the most flow between them. Where organisations or flows are complex, this may require sophisticated computer programs.

Designing the best product layout, however, requires trying to find the most efficient linked-up materials flow. The two most important elements in designing a product layout are:

- making sure all of the tasks are carried out in the correct sequence
- making sure that correct time allowances are allocated to all of the tasks assigned to different workstations (work areas).

If the time allocated to the tasks at a particular workstation is not long enough, that workstation or server will start to fall behind – creating a bottleneck in the process. For example, consider a cafeteria line as shown in Figure 2.5 where the worker serving the vegetables is much slower than the person serving the puddings. A queue of people waiting for vegetables will start to build up, while the person serving puddings has little to do. By calculating the cycle times for each activity, and considering the sequence of activities, the line can be balanced so that flow is as smooth as possible.

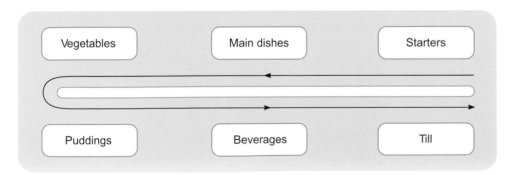

Figure 2.5: Cafeteria floor plan

A product layout is very different from a process layout. As we have seen, in a process layout similar activities are grouped together. Although this helps focus what goes on within different activity areas, the distance that products or customers have to travel within the transformation process may be very long compared with a product focus. In a factory, you might find three different kinds of assembly lines in a product-focused layout: Ushaped, straight or branching, depending on the variety of the product and the division of tasks between workers and equipment.

The cell layout attempts to combine features of both the process and the product layouts, by grouping products or customers with similar processing requirements, identifying their flow patterns and grouping activities into cells. So, for example, in a furniture factory, an organisation might move from either a process layout (where sawing, turning and sanding operations are each organised into departments and brought together in assembly) or a product layout (where dining tables, desks and computer tables are produced on separate assembly lines) to a cell layout: one cell is allocated to legs and another to tops, and the two are brought together in assembly.

Organising flow through the layout

As well as layout, which allocates different activities to specific locations, process design also involves the flow of materials, information and people between these locations. Materials or customer flow describes how these physical inputs will travel between different activities, including where they will be stored between them. Information flow describes how information will flow either in the same direction as the physical material or customer flow (e.g., information about what processes have already happened or will happen next) or in the direction opposite to the physical flow (e.g., feedback to earlier processes about changes or improvements).

We can identify two different ways of organising the flow of materials, information or customers through the operations process, according to whether the system is process focused or product focused.

In 'process-focused operations', the emphasis is on the flexibility of the process in order to produce customised goods or services for customers. For example, in a supermarket the flow of customers can be described as process focused, that is, customers can map their own path through the system in order to minimise the time spent in unnecessary activities and focus on the areas that they wish to visit. Similarly, in a garage, each vehicle might follow a different route as it is being repaired. We can describe the flow in each of these situations as 'jumbled' – the materials, information or customers being transformed can take many different paths between activities. Figure 2.6 shows an example of the different paths customers can take in a sandwich shop.

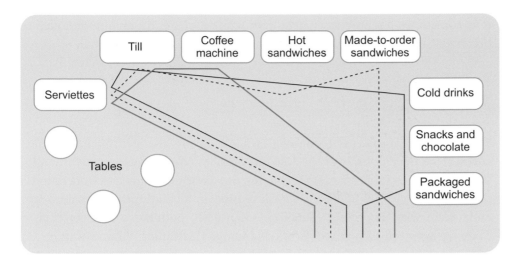

Figure 2.6: Layout of a sandwich shop

In 'product-focused operations', the emphasis is on standardising the process in order to produce standardised outputs at the lowest possible cost. Products that are produced using assembly lines, such as consumer electronics, follow a single predetermined route through the factory. Some types of services, such as mass immunisation, use a similar approach to the flow of consumers through the system. In product-focused operations, flows are described as line flows, because there is only a single path between activities for materials, information or customers.

In Figure 2.6, it is fairly easy to see how different layouts apply for the movement of materials or the movement of customers. There are some cases, however, where identifying layout and flow is more difficult. Think about trying to purchase a good or service over the internet. Some internet sites have a predetermined path that customers (or potential customers) must follow in order to find out information or to purchase a product. Others, such as Amazon (www.amazon.co.uk), allow customers to take many different paths through the site. For e-retailers the design of their websites is a key issue, since as many as 80 per cent of visitors who commence the purchasing process give up before they get to the checkout.

Stop and reflect

Visit some e-retailing websites and see whether they are product focused or process focused. Which of these do you think works best for the type of product being offered? Bear in mind that a product focus is likely to be best for standardised products and a process focus best for customised products.

Once a layout has been installed it may be very difficult and costly to change, especially if this will require building work or moving heavy equipment. Changing the layout of a retail store or supermarket, for example, will usually mean a period of closure or at best considerable disruption. This is bound to lead to loss of trade. On the other hand, the wrong layout will waste time and money, for example through making customers or materials travel more than necessary, without adding any value.

It is sometimes possible to change flow without changing layout, although the extent of changes will be constrained.

2.2: Process technologies

The evolution of **process technologies** has radically changed manufacturing and service operations over the last few decades. Nowadays, practically all organisations use some sort of technology in their operations. As operations managers are also involved in managing process technologies, they need to understand what emerging technologies can do to optimise their operations. They do not need to be experts in computing, electronics, engineering or whatever technology they use or would like to use in their companies, but they must have a good understanding of the functionalities and the immediate technological context in which process technologies are used so that they will be able to evaluate the benefits for operations when dealing with experts.

In this section, we will introduce some important concepts related to the adoption of technology in operations. After defining process technology and its two general types, we will present the three different categories of process technologies. Each category will be illustrated with specific technologies that are commonly used by organisations. These technologies will be described in terms of their functionalities, the main organisational benefits they promote and the constraining aspects they impose.

After studying this section, you should be able to:

- define the main types of process technologies
- critically appraise organisational factors influencing the choice of process technologies
- discuss the impact of process technologies on operations.

What is process technology?

In general, the term 'technology' usually refers to material objects such as machines, utensils and devices that are of use to humans. The term also encompasses immaterial things such as systems, methods and techniques that can be applied to help achieve particular goals. From a business perspective, companies can either embed technology in their goods or services or use technology to support their production and delivery (Brown et al., 2001). Process technology refers to this latter form of technology usage. Therefore, process technology can be defined as the equipment, machine, device or system that helps the creation and/or delivery of goods and services (Slack et al., 2007).

Some process technologies contribute directly to the production and delivery of goods and services (Harrison, 1996). For example, a coating machine that uses a precise amount of chocolate to make a chocolate bar is contributing directly to the production of the final product. This technology is called **direct process technology**.

Companies can also use technologies that assist in the production process rather than contribute directly to the creation and delivery of goods and services. This type of technology is peripheral to the actual creation of goods and services, but it plays an important role in facilitating and supporting the infrastructure for those processes that directly contribute to their creation and delivery (Slack and Lewis, 2002). Examples include computer systems which run stock control systems and can be used to help managers control and improve the operations. This type of technology is called **indirect process technology** and it is particularly useful in helping to manage and support activities. Figure 2.7 situates these two general types of process technology in the transformation model of operations.

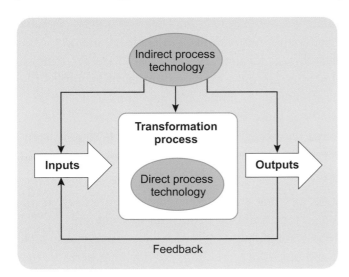

Figure 2.7: Direct and indirect process technology

Stop and reflect

Think about the different types of technologies used in your organisation. Which ones could be considered direct process technologies? And which could be considered indirect process technologies?

Materials-, information- and customer-processing technologies

Process technologies can be classified according to the category of the inputs they process. Companies can process materials, information or customers, so process technologies can be classified as either **materials-processing technologies**, **information-processing technologies** or **customer-processing technologies**. This classification helps us to understand the functionalities of different process technologies.

Current technologies integrate functionalities for processing combinations of materials, information and customers at the same time. For example, when customers take their shopping to a supermarket cashier, the purchasing process is carried out by a technology called Electronic Point of Sale (**EPOS**), which can process customers by adding up the value of their purchases as well as process information by updating stock records of the items sold. In reality, so many different processing technologies are used in operations that it would be impossible to cover all of them here. Also, more advanced technologies are constantly being developed. Regardless of the process technology, however, they were all developed with the purpose of processing materials, information or customers, or a combination of these, to support the production of goods or the delivery of services.

Materials-processing technologies

Materials-processing technologies are technologies that process one or more types of material such as chemicals, fabric, metals, plastics, etc. The operations activities that these technologies can perform involve material transformation (transformation of raw materials into finished goods), material movement (movement of materials from one place to another) and/or material storage (automated storage, location and retrieval of stored items). Materials-processing technologies are more commonly used in manufacturing than in services. Industrial robots, for example, are most commonly used in factories. Although the details of these technologies involve more engineering than management knowledge, operations managers should have a good understanding of the most common ones. The two examples below represent classic materials-processing technologies.

Robots – are machines or devices that can be programmed to perform a variety of tasks. In operations, they are used mainly for moving and manipulating materials. Robots are suitable performing repetitive tasks, such as paint spraying, loading and unloading, welding, etc. for long periods. In many applications, particularly those in the car industry, they are programmed once and then repeat the same task for years. Although robots cannot perform tasks that require sophisticated judgement and sensory feedback, they are especially useful in reaching places that are difficult for humans to reach or for handling hazardous substances, such as hot steel ingots, explosives or radioactive materials.

Flexible manufacturing systems – a **flexible manufacturing system** (FMS) is where separate machines or devices are under the control of a central computer that coordinates the operations and finds the best timetables for specific tasks (Waters, 2002). The central computer also controls the movement of materials between machines. Once an FMS is programmed, the system can work with very little human intervention. The functionalities mentioned here provide a number of advantages to an FMS.

- It can work continuously and consistently, allowing high scale and quality.
- It allows high flexibility in managing manufacturing resources, such as time and effort.
- Due to its flexibility, an FMS is able to perform different actions in case of changes.
- The high utilisation of resources allows low operating costs.

Despite these benefits, there are some disadvantages to an FMS:

- It is expensive to buy and set up.
- It needs programming skills.

- FMS systems are designed to match current production, so major product changes might cause problems.

Information-processing technologies

Information technology (IT) comprises any machine, device, method or system that collects, converts, stores, retrieves and/or distributes information (Harrison, 1996). In practice, IT involves the use of computers and devices (hardware) as well as computer programs or applications (software) that are combined together to form information systems that can securely process information. The integration of electronic communication technologies into computers has considerably increased the networking capabilities of IT and sometimes people use the abbreviation ICT (information and communications technology) when referring to IT.

IT is changing many aspects of operations, improving the efficiency of some and allowing new operations that were previously impossible.

Currently, the number of IT applications is so vast that it would be impractical to describe all of them in this book. Here are two examples of IT-based developments that have caused substantial impacts on organisations' operations:

- The internet – undoubtedly, the internet is the most significant information technology to impact on operations management. In practice, the internet is a worldwide, publicly accessible network of computers. It connects millions of academic, business, government and smaller domestic networks, which together carry various types of information and services, such as email, file transfer, online chat and the interlinked web pages and other resources of the world wide web (WWW). These functionalities have allowed the creation of many innovative operations in the past and there will certainly be many more innovations to come in the future.

- Electronic business (**e-business**) – can be understood as any business process that relies on internet-based technology. By improving existing processes or creating entirely new business opportunities, companies are linking their internal and external information systems to work more closely with customers, suppliers and partners. One of the most considerable impacts has been on those operations and business processes that involve buying and selling activities. This business model is known as **e-commerce**.

However, e-business is more than just e-commerce, which can be seen as a subset of an overall e-business strategy. Often, e-business involves the provision of services as well as the application of knowledge management systems to build and enhance relationships with stakeholders. The cost of transactions conducted through the internet is significantly lower than the cost of transactions through other channels of communication. Figure 2.8 shows the relative cost to a retail bank of providing its services through different channels. With cost savings of this scale, internet-based services have become the preferred medium for many operations.

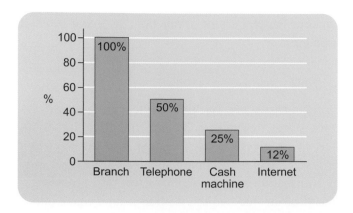

Figure 2.8: Relative cost of service delivery per channel (a retail bank) (Source: Slack et al., 2007, p. 231)

Customer-processing technologies

Customer-processing technologies are customer-driven technologies. They are the main type of technology used by many service firms. There are two types of customer-processing technologies: those directly operated by the customers and those operated by an intermediary. For example, when booking theatre tickets, a customer can either make the reservation by interacting directly with an internet-based system or have an intermediary to do it for them – for example, a booking agent.

Two examples illustrating common customer-processing technologies are described below.

- In-flight entertainment – this type of technology allows customers to interact with personalised terminals at the passenger's seat linked to a central processor. By operating the terminals themselves, the customers can choose between a range of entertainment services such as film, television, radio and news. This gives the customers something to keep them busy and reduces the role of the cabin attendants.

- Moving walkways – these are technologies that transport a large number of customers over short distances through simple moving belts driven from under the floor. They are particularly helpful in airports in improving punctuality, speeding up the flow of passengers through the terminals.

Choice of technology

Stop and reflect

How can you choose adequate types of process technologies for your organisation?

Making decisions concerning which technology to choose is a common situation that operations managers face. Such decisions usually involve choices between alternative technologies and variants of the same technology. The complexity of these decisions may vary from simple technology upgrades to more difficult decisions with long-term impact on the operations strategy and capability.

Complex technology choices are generally based on three important evaluation perspectives:

- market requirement evaluation, which takes into account the importance of satisfying customer needs

- operations resource evaluation, which focuses on building operations capabilities

- financial evaluation, which assesses the financial value of the investment on technology.

Market requirement evaluation is about evaluating the potential impact of a process technology on the operations' ability to fulfil customer needs. A useful framework for this sort of evaluation is to assess how a specific technology would affect the performance of the operations in terms of quality, speed, dependability, flexibility and cost. The example below illustrates the market requirement evaluation for a warehouse that stores, packs and distributes spare parts to its customers (Slack et al., 2007).

A market requirement evaluation for a warehouse's technology choice

A warehouse is considering investing in a new 'retrieval and packing' system which converts sales orders into 'retrieval lists' and uses materials-handling equipment to automatically pick up the goods from its shelves and bring them to the packing area. The market requirements evaluation for this technology choice could be as follows:

- *Quality*: The impact on quality could be the fact that the computerised system is not prone to human error, which may previously have resulted in the wrong part being picked off the shelves.

- *Speed*: The new system may be able to retrieve items from the shelves faster than human operators can do safely.

- *Dependability*: This will depend on how reliable the new system is. If it is less likely to break down than the operators in the old system were likely to be absent, then the new system may improve the dependability of the service.

- *Flexibility*: New service flexibility is not likely to be as good as the previous manual system. For example, there will be a physical limit to the size of the products the automatic system will be able to retrieve, whereas people are capable of adapting to doing new things in new ways. Volume flexibility, however, could be better. The new system can work for longer hours when demand is higher than expected or deadlines are changed.

> • *Cost*: The new system is likely to require fewer operators for the warehouse, but will need extra technical and maintenance support. Overall, however, labour costs are likely to be lower.
>
> (Source: Slack et al., 2007, p. 241)

Operations resource evaluation is about assessing the potential (or capabilities) that a new process technology will bring to the organisation, as well as its effects (or constraints) on the operations. Thus, this sort of evaluation usually includes two dimensions: assessment of the capabilities enabled by the process technology being considered and assessment of the constraints the process technology may impose on the operations. For example, a technology that automates the production of a specific good may increase the volume capability of the operation. However, the same technology may impose a variety of constraints on the operations if it does not have the flexibility to produce goods with different specifications such as size, colour and shape.

Finally, *financial evaluation* is about assessing the financial value of investing in a specific process technology.

The three perspectives mentioned above (market, operations and finance) can also be considered in an evaluation framework that takes into account the *feasibility*, *acceptability* and *vulnerability* of the process technology being assessed. Feasibility refers to the difficulties involved in acquiring the technology; acceptability refers to the benefits the technology will bring to the organisation; and vulnerability refers to the risks involved in acquiring the technology. The framework, shown in Table 2.2 below, provides a useful reference to support technology choice, as it gives managers evaluation criteria based on the relevant perspectives and dimensions described above. In practice, it allows managers to generate initial insights that will help them to make their decision on whether or not to adopt a process technology.

Table 2.2: Evaluation criteria framework for technology choice

Feasibility	Acceptability	Vulnerability
How difficult is it?	How worthwhile is it?	What could go wrong?
Do we have the skills to acquire the new technology?	Does the option satisfy market requirements?	What are the risks involved?
Do we have the financial resources to purchase it?	Will our customers want it?	Can we carry on running if things go wrong?
Do we have adequate facilities/capacity?	Does the option give a satisfactory financial return?	Do we understand the full consequences of adopting the option?

(Source: adapted from Slack et al., 2007, p. 127)

2.3: Planning and control

Planning and **control** are core tasks of all managers. In operations management, planning and control are necessary for the operation to run efficiently and effectively, and to produce the goods or services required by customers in the appropriate quantity, at the appropriate time and at the appropriate level of quality. The main goal of a planning and control system is to match the potential of the operation to supply goods and services with the demands of its customers or clients for those goods and services.

After studying this section, you should be able to:

- understand the nature of operations planning and control
- identify and apply relevant operations planning and control practices, tools and techniques
- describe operations management practices to manage demand and capacity
- explain why inventory is necessary for organisations.

The nature of planning and control

The operations function is a planned process that usually involves different resources and people performing various actions for the achievement of a determined objective. In operations management, plans relate to a number of different time frames – long term, medium term and short term:

- Organisations make *long-term* plans for the total capacity needed to produce their outputs, often over a period of five to ten years into the future. These are sometimes called 'aggregate capacity' plans. For example, a car assembly plant might make long-term plans for the total number of cars to be produced in the future, rather than the numbers of individual models. Similarly, a hospital might make plans for the total number of beds available, rather than for the maternity ward, intensive care unit, and so on. To support this level of planning, the operations function needs to plan the number and location of its facilities, as well as investment in major capital equipment.

- *Medium-term* planning involves making resources available to meet the requirements of the long-term plan. It typically concerns a period of two to five years into the future. For many organisations, the long **lead times** involved in building or acquiring facilities and/or specialised equipment mean that these resources are relatively inflexible over a shorter period. A medium-term operations plan breaks down the aggregate capacity plan into time periods, resource categories and types of good or service, to show how operations will meet the forecast demands for goods or services.

- In the *short term*, the operations function needs to have a detailed schedule of all the activities that will be required to achieve its objectives over the next one or two years. During this period, it is likely that priorities will need to be changed and activities rescheduled to deal with unexpected variations from the plan. For example, on a day-to-day basis operations may have to respond to a higher or lower demand for goods or services, disruptions to the supply of inputs or breakdowns in machines and equipment. It is at this point that planning moves into control. In this sense, operations managers are much like anyone else. For example, if you drive to work, you probably have a predetermined (planned) route that you take every day. Occasionally, however, you may have to make a detour to deal with road works or avoid heavy traffic (control).

As we move from the long term to the short term, the focus of operations management shifts from planning to control. While operations planning is concerned with acquiring and managing all the resources needed to support the production of goods or services in the future, operations control is concerned with implementing plans and adjusting all aspects of the work to make sure that the operations plan is achieved. Planning results in a formal statement of intentions, while control deals with variations from a plan. Planning is concerned mainly with providing adequate levels of resources (inputs) to the transformation process to create outputs, taking account of expected changes in technology and shifts in the demand for the organisation's goods or services. Control is concerned with meeting demand and utilising resources in the best way possible on a day-to-day basis.

A model for operations planning is shown in Figure 2.9. Note that planning and control by the operations function must take into account the strategic decisions made at a higher level in the organisation and coordinate with the decisions made in other functional areas, such as marketing and finance. These decisions are not under the control of the operations function, although operations may have some influence on them.

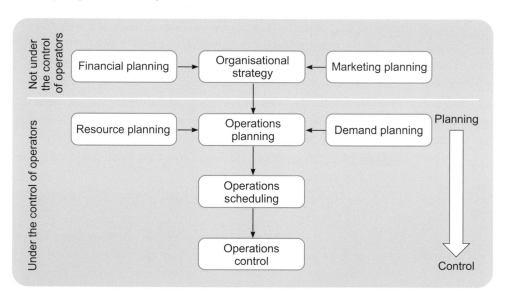

Figure 2.9: The context of operations planning and control

Within small operations, planning and control tasks may be relatively informal processes. In large organisations, however, they must be highly formalised in order to ensure effective coordination, and they are often based on computer systems that can handle the large quantity of information involved. Lack of effective operations planning almost inevitably leads to higher costs as a result of unnecessarily high levels of stock, poor customer service, excess capacity, longer lead times, decisions being made on an ad hoc basis rather than guided by strategic considerations, and inadequate responses to environmental changes or new opportunities.

Stop and reflect

Think about the organisation you work for or one you are familiar with. Can you recognise any planning or control processes in it?

Managing capacity and demand

One of the main planning and control responsibilities of operations managers is managing the capacity of the operation. Decisions about capacity are strategic in nature, often involving a trade-off between (a) the risk of selecting a level of capacity that is too low to meet the demand for the organisation's outputs, and (b) the risk of wasting investment in resources by selecting a level of capacity that is too high.

The key steps in capacity planning and control are:

- understanding and measuring the level of – and fluctuations in – the capacity of the operation to produce outputs
- understanding and measuring the level of – and fluctuations in – the demand for the operation's outputs
- establishing a strategy for matching capacity and demand.

The goal of capacity planning is to match the available level of facilities, equipment and human resources to the predicted level of demand for the organisation's goods or services.

Measuring capacity

An organisation's capacity is the volume of goods or services that it can deliver to its customers or clients under normal operating conditions during a given time period. The way an organisation defines and measures its capacity has a considerable influence on how this capacity is managed.

The two major factors that affect capacity are the capability of the organisation's transformation process and the throughput of that process. For many organisations, capacity is therefore expressed in terms of the available staff and/or facilities and equipment, because the level of materials, information or customers to be processed can be varied more easily. In some operations, such as a management consultancy or a firm of accountants, the factor limiting their capacity is the availability of skilled personnel to provide the service, with facilities and equipment required mostly just to enable their work. This is often the case for operations that provide one-off or very small quantities of specialised outputs. In such operations, staff hours usually determine their capacity.

In operations that produce large quantities of standardised goods or provide standardised services to a mass market, the factor limiting capacity is the availability of facilities and equipment to produce outputs. This is the case in many manufacturing organisations, as well as in service organisations such as airlines, where the number of seats in a plane determines how many passengers can travel, or restaurants, where the number of tables and chairs limits the number of people who can eat at the same time.

Forecasting demand

All companies have some level of demand for the products (goods and/or services) they deliver. Although companies can influence the demand for their products (see 'Demand management' later in this section), they normally try to adjust their operations capacity according to the general demand for their products. For example, supermarkets, banks and retail shops try to keep a good proportion of customers per cashier so that the customers do not have to spend too much time queuing. The operations function controls this by allocating cashiers according to customer demand. Logically, they allocate more cashiers during peak times and fewer cashiers during off-peak times.

Forecasting demand is usually based on what managers know about the behaviour of their customers. Such knowledge is a very useful source of ideas about what the pattern of demand is likely to be (Galloway et al., 2000). In some cases it is possible to know what the demand for a certain good or service is going to be ahead of time – this is usually the case when customers place their orders in advance. This situation, where the demand is known prior to the delivery, is called **dependent demand**, and the planning for the delivery capacity can be done with a high degree of certainty. On the other hand, there are situations where the demand can only be estimated. This situation, where the capacity requirements are defined based on estimated demand, is termed **independent demand**, as the demand is independent of the control of the operation (Galloway et al., 2000). The box below provides an example of dependent and independent demand.

Dependent and independent demand in a hospital

Hospitals are aware of the difference between dependent and independent demand. The former is represented by elective surgery, where medical operations are booked in advance. In these cases the hospital can plan to provide the necessary capacity knowing what type and number of operations will be required. Primary care capacity, in the form of operating theatres, clinical and nursing staff, medical supplies, and beds can be allocated with a high degree of certainty. Supporting services, such as catering and laundry, can also be planned. The position with emergency surgery, i.e., independent demand, is far more difficult to plan for. If the number of emergency surgery operations exceeds the capacity of the hospital, then usually booked appointments are cancelled. This releases the necessary resources to cope, but risks causing a high level of dissatisfaction amongst those patients whose operations are cancelled at very short notice.

(Source: Galloway et al., 2000, p. 165)

Uncertainty is an inherent feature of demand. Even in a dependent demand scenario, where companies know in advance the demand for goods and services, there is always a degree of uncertainty regarding what is going to be the actual demand. The example above shows how independent demand (emergency surgeries) affects dependent demand (booked surgeries). Nonetheless, dependent demand is always preferable to independent demand, as the delivery capacity can be better planned. Although it is not always possible, companies try to move from 'forecasts' to 'known' orders whenever they can so that the uncertainty of the demand can be minimised. This is one of the many ways in which companies can manage demand.

Sales and/or marketing managers are usually involved with demand forecasting. Simply put, **forecasting demand** is the estimate of future demand for goods or services delivered by an organisation. This information is very important for operations managers. It is based upon forecasting information that they can adjust and allocating the necessary resources for delivering their goods or services in advance in a more efficient and effective manner. In other words, organisations need to forecast demand in order to properly determine their capacity requirements for the future (Hill, 2005) – therefore, forecasting demand is critical for planning capacity. Companies that do not have an estimate of future demand cannot plan effectively for future events; they can only react to them (Slack et al., 2007).

A forecast is a statement of what is expected to happen in the future. From a management perspective, it is aimed at identifying variations or fluctuations in demand that usually have seasonality patterns. Due to the changing nature of markets, there will always be a degree of uncertainty in demand forecasting. In addition, although seasonal demand fluctuations are reasonably predictable, they may be affected by unexpected variations in the weather and changing economic conditions (Slack et al., 2007). For example, the sales of ice-cream, sunglasses, sun lotions, waterproof clothing, etc. are strongly affected by the weather. Typically, the seasonality of demand occurs over the period of a year. However, there are many businesses in which shorter seasonality cycles are also taken into account. For instance, supermarkets, banks, telecommunication providers, utility companies and public transport companies usually have weekly, daily and even hourly variation in demand patterns that require capacity adjustment.

The demand for goods and services is also affected by the actions of competitors, as well as by development of the goods or services being offered. The latter may require an understanding of where the good or service is located in its life cycle – demand changes as a product moves through the phases of introduction, growth, maturity and decline (Figure 2.10).

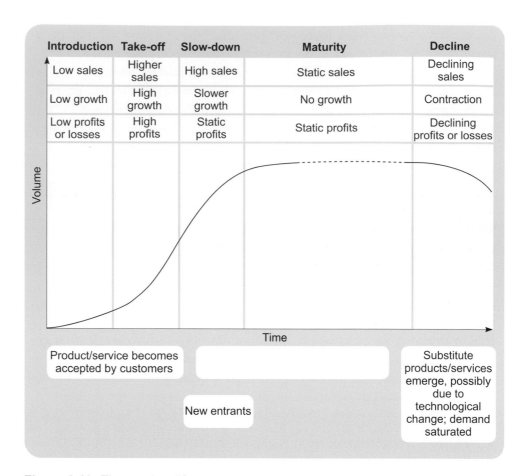

Figure 2.10: The product life cycle

Stop and reflect

How can organisations cope with demand fluctuation?

Strategies for matching capacity and demand

As well as matching capacity and demand in the long term, organisations need to plan to make the best possible use of their existing capacity to meet demand in the medium and short terms. Levels of demand may be affected by short-term fluctuations, such as the season (e.g., ice-cream, bathing costumes), the day of the week (e.g., religious observances, schools) and the time of day (e.g., public transport, coffee shops), as well as by marketing and promotional activities.

Two general strategies for matching capacity and demand in the medium term are **level capacity** (keeping capacity constant despite demand fluctuations) and **chase demand** (adjusting capacity to meet demand). It is sometimes possible to use a third strategy, **demand management** (changing demand to match capacity). These strategies are explained further below.

Level capacity

A 'level capacity' strategy means continuing to operate at the same level, no matter what the level of customer demand. The level of capacity can be set at the maximum expected level of customer demand (emergency services are expected to do this), the minimum expected level (many public services) or some level in between. The advantage of this strategy is that it reduces the need to make changes in levels of activity. This helps to minimise operating costs, especially if capacity is set at the minimum level of demand. However, if capacity is set at the maximum level of demand, the resulting resources will often be under-utilised, leading to high costs and waste.

For manufacturing operations, in which products can be made when demand is lower and then stored, a level capacity strategy that aligns production with average demand may minimise costs, since finished products can be held in stock to meet above-average demand at certain times. This works particularly well for seasonal goods such as holiday merchandise. Such a strategy, however, is rarely available in service operations, since most services (e.g., hairdressing or surgery) cannot be produced and 'stored' in advance. Using a level capacity strategy in such situations often means that customers cannot be served or have to wait for service, which is likely to lead to dissatisfaction.

Chase demand

An organisation using a 'chase demand' strategy changes its output in response to changes in customer demand. This usually involves adjusting the number of staff working to produce outputs. It is a common strategy in service operations: for example, tourist attractions often hire more people during the summer, when they have more visitors. Some manufacturing operations chase demand by increasing or decreasing their volume of output, but this is often supplemented by drawing on stocks of finished products.

Chase demand strategies often include:

- hiring and firing staff

- training staff to perform more than one job

- using part-time or temporary staff

- sub-contracting on a temporary basis.

Demand management

Besides responding to demand, companies can also adjust the level of demand for their goods and services so that their delivery capacity can be managed with greater certainty. Initiatives to manage demand allow organisations to better plan their delivery capacity so that the objectives of the business and the needs of customers can align more effectively (Hill, 2005). Some of the main demand management initiatives that companies have developed are described below.

- Reserving a capacity in advance: requiring customers or clients to reserve their use of capacity in advance – such as tables at restaurants or personal services such as hairdressing – can be an effective method for controlling the use of scarce resources. These initiatives attempt to move from 'forecasts' to 'known' orders with the purpose of minimising uncertainty and maximising certainty. One of the most common practices in this area is to implement 'Reservation and appointment systems', which are systems or mechanisms that allow customers to pre-book their orders. If preferred options are already taken, these systems point out similar or alternative options available. Many companies reinforce reservation systems by advertising discounts or benefits for customers who make bookings at an early date. Although pre-booked orders provide fairly accurate information about future demand, they do not necessarily guarantee that the demand will actually happen, as customers can cancel booked reservations. To tackle this problem, many companies couple prebookings with pre-payments and establish cancellation penalties related to the numbers of days ahead of the cancellation.

- Changing the pattern of demand: these initiatives are aimed at adjusting the level or patterns of demand. Some of the main initiatives that companies adopt in order to influence the pattern or level of demand for their products (goods or services) are:

  - Price differentiation – companies frequently offer higher prices for peak and lower prices for off-peak times in order to persuade customers to choose periods when the demand level is usually low. For example, transport companies regularly offer discounts for off-peak travel, hotels regularly offer reduced prices during off-season holidays and many restaurants offer menu discounts during the early evening. Price discounts can also be used to motivate scheduling (early booking discounts).

  - Advertising – although advertising is typically used to stimulate demand for new goods and services, it can also be used to reinforce price differentiation and other initiatives aimed at stimulating demand for off-peak periods (e.g., supermarkets can advertise turkey sales outside of traditional seasons such as Christmas).

  - Complementary goods and/or services – complementary goods and services are developed with the purpose of creating alternative demand for seasonal markets, as illustrated below.

Demand management in the greetings card industry

The greetings card industry is a typical example of an industry that traditionally operates in seasonal markets. Mother's Day, Father's Day, Hallowe'en, Valentine's Day and other occasions have all been promoted as times to send (and buy) appropriately designed cards. Now, having run out of occasions to promote, greetings card manufacturers have moved on to 'non-occasion' cards, which can be sent at any time. These have the considerable advantage of being less seasonal, thus making the companies' seasonality less marked. Hallmark Cards has been the pioneer in developing non-occasion cards. Its cards include those intended to be sent from a parent to a child with messages such as 'Would a hug help?' or 'You're perfectly wonderful – it's your room that's a mess'. Other cards deal with more serious adult themes such as friendship ('You're more than a friend, you're just like family') or even alcoholism ('This is hard to say, but I think you're a much nicer person when you're not drinking'). Now Hallmark Cards has founded a 'loyalty marketing group' that helps companies communicate with their customers at an emotional level. It promotes the use of greetings cards for corporate use, to show that customer and employees are valued. Whatever else these new products may be, they are not seasonal!

(Source: adapted from Slack et al., 2007, p. 340)

Scheduling

Scheduling is concerned with matching the flow of inputs and outputs on a short-term, often day-to-day, basis. Because delivering products on time is so important to the competitiveness of operations, many different approaches to scheduling have been developed. For manufacturing operations, the main focus is on controlling the rate at which inputs are converted into outputs – known as production scheduling. In addition, there are different ways of managing customer orders. In service operations, including many not-for-profit organisations, scheduling generally means controlling the flow of customers or clients – queuing. Finally, there is the question of sequencing – deciding which customers or jobs should be scheduled first.

Production scheduling

There are two major approaches to production scheduling: **push** and **pull**. In principle, both are quite straightforward, but in practice they can be enormously complex, especially within large organisations making products with many inputs.

In push scheduling, operations managers begin with a plan for the quantity of output to be produced in some future period. They then decide what activities are required to support this target, and develop a detailed schedule of what must be done, and when. This schedule acts as a central control mechanism for every input and transformation process required. It is called a 'push' schedule because the production process is pushed through successive stages until the finished product has been completed. A problem with push scheduling is that, if difficulties arise at any stage in the production process, there is likely to be a build-up of stocks or components, or partly finished work.

In pull scheduling, production of a component or initiation of an activity is only authorised when it is needed for the next stage of the process. This is the basis of the Japanese **just-in-time** (JIT) concept, which is a central feature of the Toyota Production System. If the next process is not ready to receive any inputs, the previous process will not produce any, thus minimising the amount of just-in-case or wasted stock. If there is any disruption, the entire production process may come to a halt, but this is regarded as a lesser problem than producing faulty products or excessive unsold stock.

Managing the customer order cycle

Another aspect to consider when scheduling the output of products is to what extent inputs can be acquired and elements of the transformation process can be undertaken prior to receiving customer orders. There are three main approaches to this: **resource-to-order**, **make-to-order** and **make-to-stock**.

In resource-to-order, the operation does not acquire resources or begin work until it receives a customer order. An example of a resource-to-order operation is catering at special events, where the organisation will wait for a contract from a customer before ordering stocks of food. This minimises the chance of investing in inappropriate resources or resources that will spoil before they are used. Such a strategy is often used in the production of specialised products (e.g., building a cyclotron particle accelerator) or in major construction projects (e.g., building a bridge).

In make-to-order, resources are acquired but no work is done until a customer order is received. For example, a shop that assembles custom-made bicycles might keep a stock of frames, wheels, seats, and so on, but not assemble them into a finished bicycle until an order is received. Similarly, a sandwich shop keeps tubs of various sandwich fillings and loaves of bread, but does not assemble a sandwich until a customer orders a particular combination.

In make-to-stock, resources are acquired and all the work necessary to complete a product is performed prior to a customer order being received. For example, most stereo equipment is manufactured independently of any customer order and most supermarkets offer pre-packaged sandwiches.

Queuing

Since service operations cannot generally prepare their product in advance and store it until customers want it, the main way in which capacity and demand are matched is by creating 'stocks' of customers waiting to be served – that is, queues. This is especially important for operations where the timing of customer arrivals is not within the organisation's control. Although there are sophisticated ways of analysing queues mathematically, you cannot have failed to notice from your everyday experiences (in restaurants, supermarkets, banks and on public transport) that, in practice, customers often end up in queues.

Some of the major decisions in managing queues are:

- What level of capacity is needed to provide adequate customer service?
- How can the queue be managed to avoid a negative impact on customer satisfaction?
- How should the queue be physically managed?

Operations managers have to balance the preference of customers to be served immediately against the cost of providing enough staff and equipment to satisfy this desire. Some customers or clients will inevitably have to wait at certain times, but the aim of the service delivery system is to provide sufficient capacity so that waiting times, when unavoidable, are within acceptable limits. A commonly applied rule of thumb is that the system should be designed so that the staff who serve customers are busy for only 70 per cent of the time (and are therefore not serving customers for 30 per cent of the time). This may still result in queues, however, either because demand tends to be variable over the course of the day or week, or because service times tend to differ due to the different tasks performed for each customer.

Not surprisingly, studies of customer satisfaction show that queuing tends to have negative impacts: customers experience boredom, frustration, anger or anxiety, which they will associate with the organisation. If customers seeking a service see a long queue ahead of them, they may either 'baulk' (refuse to join it) or 'renege' (leave the queue before they are served). In either case, their business may be permanently lost to the organisation, especially if there are competitors.

The design of a queuing system can make the queue work for or against customer satisfaction. Four commonly used queuing systems are shown in Figure 2.11. In system A, customers or clients form a single queue to wait for a single server. In systems C and D, customers form either a single queue or multiple queues to wait for multiple servers. Although the length of a single queue for multiple servers appears longer than multiple queues would, it has the advantage of appearing to move faster, since it moves more often. It is also seen to be more equitable: we have all had the experience of choosing the slowest-moving queue and watching people in other queues get served faster. In system B, the customer-processing operation is arranged as a series of queues. At an airport, for example, passengers queue to get a boarding pass, go through security and passport control, board the plane, and so on. Sequential queuing systems need to be designed to avoid 'queuing overload' among customers or clients; the aim should be to minimise the time spent at each server and maximise the efficiency of each individual phase. Similar queuing systems are also used in operations such as call-centres, where customers are held in electronic queues while they wait to talk to an operator.

If queues are unavoidable, it may be possible to design them to entertain or inform customers or clients while they are waiting. Some organisations show videos to customers standing in queues or allow them to observe part of the operations.

Queues can also be used as an opportunity to get customers or clients to do productive work. For example, customers standing in a restaurant queue can read the menu and decide what they want before they are seated, and a doctor's surgery may get patients to fill in forms while they are waiting to be seen. In some organisations, queues are used to encourage customers to purchase additional goods or services, such as retailers that put displays of items often purchased on impulse adjacent to the tills.

Some organisations also engage in 'queue combing'. Staff walk down queues checking on customer needs to see if they can be better served in another way. Airlines often do this with check-in queues to identify passengers checking in late for flights that are soon to depart. Some banks comb queues to redirect customers who can be more quickly served at a cash machine or by enquiries staff rather than cashiers.

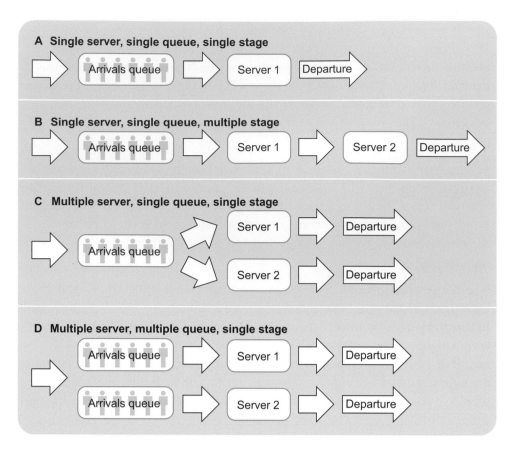

Figure 2.11: Different queuing arrangements

Sequencing

Sequencing is concerned with assigning priority to tasks. The operations function can set priorities for the order in which customers or clients are dealt with, or tasks are performed, in a variety of ways.

Most service operations use 'first-come, first-served' as a way of deciding who will be served first, especially in high-contact service operations. This is generally perceived to be the fairest approach – you will often find it in use at the photocopying machine, where it is likely to be favoured by the person who arrived ahead of you! An alternative, however, is 'shortest processing time' – dealing first with the customer who can be served most quickly. This maximises the rate of work flow and equipment utilisation, which is why people waiting to use the photocopying machine often recommend this rule. A third approach is 'customer priority', in which the customer with the most urgent needs gets served first. This is the rule used, for example, in hospitals' accident and emergency departments, where the most critically ill patients take priority even if they arrive later.

Which sequencing rule an operation should use depends on what is most important – using machines or staff efficiently, getting jobs done on time or getting jobs done quickly.

Inventory management

Inventory management is an important issue in most, if not all, operations. People often tend to think that inventory is only an issue in materials processing operations, such as manufacturing. However, many service operations also use materials within their operations, and many services have physical products that form part of their outputs. Most services also use materials within their transformation processes, even if those materials form no part of their output supplied to customers. There are different kinds of inventory and some kinds of stock are more important than others.

Stop and reflect

Why is inventory necessary?

In essence, inventory exists to compensate for the differences in timing between supply and demand. A key dilemma at the heart of inventory management is concerned with how much stock an organisation should hold: organisations will want to avoid the high costs of holding too much, but will want to avoid losing output (and potential loss of income) that could result from having too little. The level of stock an organisation holds will be affected by decisions about what quantities of materials to order from suppliers and by the timing of those orders. Operations managers have devised a number of different inventory management techniques and systems to help them address these decisions.

The nature of inventory

From an operations management perspective, 'inventory' generally refers to the stored accumulation (stock) of resources that are necessary in a specific transformation system (operation). Manufacturing companies usually hold stocks of the materials required for the production of their goods. Similarly, service companies typically hold 'stocks' of the customers they serve in the form of information – that is, customer databases. Intangible resources such as 'information' can also be the main transformed resource 'stocked' by companies, as in the case of accounting or tax offices.

In practice, all companies have some sort of resources stored as inventory. This is because of the imbalance between the rates of supply and demand. In order to compensate for this imbalance, companies usually hold specific inventories to keep their operations running without disruption.

Although inventory plays an important role in many operations, there are disadvantages associated with holding inventory. Some of these are:

- storage, administrative and insurance costs for the inventory
- inventory may become obsolete, be damaged or deteriorate over time
- inventory uses space that could be used by adding-value processes.

A challenge that operations managers face is to match supply and demand rates in order to keep inventory at a minimum level. As orders from customers gradually deplete the inventory, orders from the operations need to be placed for replenishment of the stock. This process requires two important decisions:

- Inventory volume decisions, which are decisions about 'how much' to order. They are usually depicted as attempts to balance the costs associated with placing an order with the costs of holding stock.

- Inventory timing decisions, which are decisions about 'when' to order. These decisions are influenced by the uncertainty of demand. In practice, replenishment orders are timed to allow a certain average safety stock whose level depends on the variability of demand and the lead time of supply.

2.4: Supply chain management

No operation can exist in isolation. All operations, irrespective of their context (manufacturing or services, for-profit or not-for-profit), have suppliers from whom they acquire their resource inputs and customers to whom they supply their outputs. Many organisations outsource parts of their operations. This process is usually accompanied by a blurring of organisational boundaries and by much closer working relationships between buyers and suppliers. Consequently, there must be a growing attention to managing operations across organisational boundaries. **Supply chain** management is concerned with operations that involve continuing relationships across organisational boundaries. All organisations exist within a set of supply relationships that include all of the activities required to create and deliver products (goods and/or services) to the end customer. Supply chain management takes a systems perspective by considering the totality of those relationships from, for example, the suppliers' suppliers to the customers' customers.

Earlier in this book, you read about the systems perspective upon which much of operations management thinking is based. In this section, we will apply an open systems perspective to operations management by emphasising the effects of the external environment on the operations. This is in contrast to much of operations management thinking, which tends to emphasise the internal organisational context of operations. Just as biological organisms must exchange resources and outputs with the external environment to survive and grow, operations must also acquire inputs and provide outputs beyond their own boundaries. Thus, from an operations perspective, supply chain management refers to the process of acquiring inputs from suppliers to be used in the transformation processes and distributing these outputs to the customers.

While many operations take place mainly within the organisation, most operations will involve relationships that cross organisational boundaries to other external units or other organisations. Even if the supply relationships of the operation in which you work are entirely within a single organisation, you can apply this way of thinking to these **internal suppliers** and **internal customers**. Furthermore, if you look at the suppliers to these internal suppliers, and the customers of these internal customers, at some point these relationships will cross the boundaries of the organisation. Even the most vertically integrated organisations have to deal with some external suppliers and customers.

Much of the academic study of supply chain management encompasses topics often covered when looking at purchasing, materials management, logistics and customer service management. In this section we will introduce the fundamental principles and some of the key aspects of supply chain management.

After studying this section, you should be able to:

- understand the full scope of a supply chain
- describe the main supply chain management functions
- explain how logistics and supply chain management can reduce organisational costs and add value for the customer.

The supply network

Simply put, the term 'supply network' refers to 'the network of suppliers and customers that have a relationship with an operation' (Slack et al., 2007). The term 'supply chain' is also used in this context. However, 'supply network' better conveys the greater degree of complexity that represents the relationships that typically exist in most organisations.

Studying the supply network is important because it sets the consideration of an operation in its wider operating context. The consideration of the supply network has become increasingly important in recent years as there has been a tendency for organisations to outsource more of their activities. Much of this outsourcing has been directed at suppliers whose operations are located in countries far away from the purchasers of their goods and services. There has also been a trend for organisations to reduce the number of suppliers they deal with in order to work more closely with their preferred suppliers.

There have also been other changes in supply networks as organisations have sought to capitalise on the opportunities offered by internet technology. For instance, the internet has allowed many companies to 'cut out the middleman' and deal directly with their customers, a business strategy known as disintermediation. This has led to the reconfiguration of many supply networks. However, many new kinds of intermediaries have also emerged. With these new dynamics emerging, it has never been more important to study the operations function from a supply network perspective.

From a functional perspective, a 'supply chain' involves the flow of materials from original supplier to end customer. Figure 2.12 presents a conceptual model of the supply chain, beginning with raw materials and ending with the receipt of the final product by customers or clients. These raw materials go through one or more production plants, from which they are distributed through distribution centres and warehouses to the end customers. Note especially the stocking points, representing the storage and consolidation of materials at different stages.

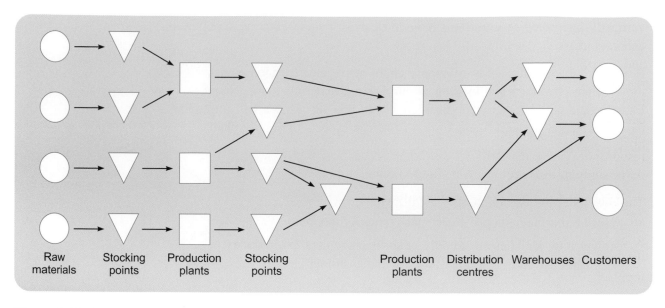

| Raw materials | Stocking points | Production plants | Stocking points | | Production plants | Distribution centres | Warehouses | Customers |

Figure 2.12: A conceptual model of a supply chain

The concept can be applied equally well to services, where the chain may also involve the flow of customers and information.

In practice, supply chain management integrates all the activities performed in purchasing, materials management, physical distribution, logistics and customer service, in order to direct them towards satisfying customer needs. The goals of supply chain management are to provide customers with outputs that are right the first time and delivered quickly and punctually at the lowest possible cost.

Stop and reflect

Think about the organisation you work for or an organisation you are familiar with. Who are the main suppliers of your organisation? What do managers working with supply chain management do?

Supply chain management activities

Supply chain management activities encompass the acquisition, storage and movement of resources within an organisation and between the organisation and its environment. These activities are fundamental to operations management. It would be useful at this point to look back at the transformation model of operations, which underpins much of the operations perspective (Figure 1.2, chapter 1).

At the starting point of the model are the resources that form the inputs to the transformation process. Some of these resources are used to perform the transformation processes, while others are themselves being transformed. Finally, the outputs produced are made available to the customers. Supply chain management is concerned with how these inputs are acquired as well as how the outputs are supplied to the customers.

Some transforming resources need be acquired only once, such as the land and buildings that form the organisation's physical facilities. Decisions about their acquisition typically involve long lead times and large amounts of capital. Therefore, they tend to be made at high levels of the organisation and are often assessed against the organisation's strategic objectives. This may also be true for the other physical assets used in the transformation process, typically equipment, machinery and information technology. These can be very expensive, not only in manufacturing but also in service operations – for example, the diagnostic equipment used in hospitals. The resources to be transformed, on the other hand, must generally be acquired on a continual basis to supply the transformation process.

The outputs from the transformation process that are supplied to customers are also the concern of supply chain management. The operation will want to ensure that these outputs are delivered in a way that meets the needs of the customer, for whose own supply chain they may well constitute the inputs.

The successful management of inputs and the distribution of outputs is vital to all organisations. Without this, the organisation would quickly fail, starved of inputs and unable to deliver their outputs. This is why many organisations have specialised groups or functional areas to manage these activities. Supply chain management activities often encompass work in the categories of purchasing, materials management, and physical distribution and logistics.

Purchasing

In large organisations **purchasing** is often a separate department or function. In smaller organisations it may simply be part of the portfolio of roles carried out by one or more employees.

The activities involved in acquiring material inputs are usually performed by purchasing, which may also be responsible for acquiring other transformed and transforming inputs, information and services. Purchasing should ensure that inputs are of the right quality, are available when needed and have an appropriate cost. Because they translate directly into financial performance figures, any cost savings achieved by purchasing can significantly affect how well the whole operation performs.

Purchasing will seek to achieve the specified quality level either through inspecting incoming goods or services, or through careful selection and certification of suppliers. In particular, organisations that have adopted all or part of a JIT approach will need to find partners who can deliver small quantities, of perfect quality, just in time and at frequent intervals. This often means dealing with suppliers who are located close by or who can themselves demonstrate excellence in supply chain management. Purchasing responsibilities are generally considered to end once the purchased inputs have been delivered.

Materials management

Materials management is responsible for the activities that take place between the delivery of materials by suppliers and their use in the transformation process. Materials management manages the receipt of incoming materials, their storage and handling and their provision to the transformation process. Once the transformation process has taken place, materials management may also be responsible for testing, packaging and storing finished products before they are shipped out of the production facility.

Outputs of the production process may go directly to customers, as in most service operations, or travel through a complex network of wholesalers, retailers and other intermediaries. In general, physical outputs must be distributed to customers either by transporting them (the most common solution for manufacturing organisations) or by locating a production facility close to consumers (the most common solution for service organisations). In project-based organisations, location decisions are often determined by the need to work on the project at a fixed site.

Organisations whose outputs are mainly goods can either locate production at a single site (e.g., to take advantage of economies of scale and lower costs from producing at higher volumes) or locate production in multiple sites (e.g., in order to locate production closer to the customer or to benefit from specialisation at each site). For example, a biscuit manufacturer might decide to concentrate its biscuit production at a single facility and its cream production at another facility, or to produce both biscuits and cream at both. Similarly, supply activities may be organised around a single distribution centre or warehouse or multiple distribution centres or warehouses. These multi-site facility decisions can be taken at the local, regional, national and even global levels.

Physical distribution and logistics

Physical distribution is the area concerned with transporting the organisation's physical outputs, managing the movement of goods and services to customers and clients.

Logistics is an extension of physical distribution management and includes all of the processes involved in the physical distribution, both into (inbound logistics) and from (outbound logistics) the organisation, as well as associated services such as credit and insurance.

Many manufacturing and service organisations manage their own logistics. However, because few of them can create competitive advantage through logistics, more and more elements of the supply chain have been outsourced to specialist providers, known as 'third-party logistics' (3PL) firms. You are likely to be familiar with one or more hauliers (road transportation companies), even if you have only seen their vehicles on the road. You might also be familiar with one or more of the giant logistics firms, such as Federal Express, United Parcel Service (UPS), TNT or DHL, which provide global logistics services for businesses and individual customers. You might not know about other elements of the supply chain that have been outsourced, such as third-party managed warehouses. These logistics specialists often are the first to develop major innovations in supply management, which then spread to in-house logistics departments. For example, Federal Express has been the world leader in developing new information technology for tracking individual parcels, as well as its hub and bespoke network and automated warehouses.

Supply as a strategic function

Stop and reflect

How can logistics and supply chain management reduce costs and add value for customers?

We have just seen that supply chain management aims at getting a product (good or service) to the right place at the right time at the lowest cost. Acquiring inputs and distributing outputs can typically account for up to 30 per cent of the total cost of goods or services. The costs of purchased inputs have been estimated to account for up to 60 per cent of the average cost of producing goods or providing a service – much more in some organisations. Thus, purchasing can have a major impact on organisational performance figures. As a result, the role of purchasing (along with the other supply chain activities) in many organisations has been changing in recent years. At one time purchasing was mainly a low-level clerical activity, concerned with preparing purchase orders and minimising purchase costs. It is now increasingly recognised as being integral to an organisation's operations strategy and central to achieving the organisation's strategic objectives.

Reck and Long (1988) developed a four-stage model, shown in Figure 2.13, to demonstrate how purchasing can become a strategic function.

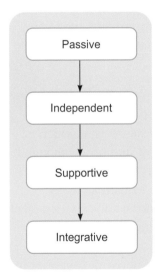

Figure 2.13: A four-stage model of purchasing
(Source: Reck and Long, 1988)

In the *passive* stage, purchasing primarily reacts to requests from other functional areas, but has no strategic direction of its own.

In the *independent* stage, purchasing has adopted strategic practices, but has not aligned these with the organisation's corporate strategy.

In the *supportive* stage, purchasing has adopted strategic practices and is supporting the organisation's corporate strategy through their use.

Finally, in the *integrative* stage, purchasing has become an integral part of the organisation's corporate strategy and is actively working with other functional areas to implement that strategy.

The model can be used to identify the current position of an organisation's purchasing function and can point the way forward for a purchasing department that is still in one of the first three stages.

While strategic supply is often associated with creating and delivering physical goods, its concepts can also be applied in many service and not-for-profit contexts.

McDonald's restaurants show how supply chain management can contribute to competitiveness in service organisations. McDonald's success is sometimes seen as being associated mainly with standardising food preparation, within each restaurant and across the world. In fact, McDonald's built much of this around radical changes to the normal restaurant supply chain, including how farmers grow potatoes and raise beef cattle. When existing major food processors refused to work to the company's specifications for hamburger meat and potatoes, McDonald's developed its own supply network. The company experimented extensively with varieties of potato and cooking techniques for French fries in order to develop the 'perfect' specification (in terms of consistency and repeatability) for suppliers. Most other restaurants concentrated on their immediate suppliers, but McDonald's managed relationships with the farmers and ranchers who provided inputs to the food processors.

The strategic potential of supply activities is not limited to profit-seeking organisations. Many government institutions – such as local council authorities, for example – work with hundreds of suppliers, ranging from small family-owned companies to large corporations, to procure everything from new buildings to equipment supplies, catering or maintenance services.

Impact of e-commerce on supply

Strategic supply has been made possible largely by developments in computer and communications technologies. Before these became widely available, most purchase orders were dispatched by post and/or telephone. During the 1980s, electronic data interchange (EDI) systems development meant that many of the routine details of transactions, as well as many routine transactions themselves, could be handled electronically. EDI enabled the whole process to be speeded up and it reduced clerical errors. However, EDI depended on the supplier having computing systems that were compatible with those of the purchaser. This usually required the supplier to make a considerable investment, which could only be recouped by the prospect of large amounts of continuing business. In this way, this technology reinforced the trend towards a smaller supplier base, with much closer and deeper relationships between the buyer and its suppliers.

The advent of the internet, however, provided the means of transforming both business-to-business (B2B) and business-to-consumer (B2C) transactions. In B2B transactions, the internet offers cheap and virtually unlimited connectivity, both within and outside the organisation, so that suppliers can be linked to any employee with access to a personal computer (PC). While this allows the delegation and dispersal of purchasing activity, it also offers the ability to aggregate more purchases, maximising volume discounts and reducing rogue buying, through online approved supplier lists and purchasing standards. Relationships with suppliers can be further deepened, encouraging more reduction in the supplier base.

However, the internet can reverse the trend to a smaller supplier base, because it offers the means of dealing with many more suppliers. Many organisations now use online reverse auctions to purchase easily specified commodity-type products. In these auctions, suppliers are invited to underbid each other, by a particular deadline, for a given quantity of goods to a certain specification. B2B e-commerce is changing traditional supply chain relationships, particularly through the creation of online exchanges. Online exchanges (also known as electronic marketplaces) act as virtual markets where suppliers go to advertise their wares and buyers purchase their requirements. They can be either horizontal (a limited range of products, for example stationery, purchased across a number of industries) or vertical (a wide range of products purchased throughout a particular industry, for example automotive parts). An example of the latter is Covisint, which was set up in 2000 as a giant electronic market by five of the world's largest car manufacturers (General Motors, Ford, Renault, DaimlerChrysler and Nissan). B2C e-commerce also has significant implications for supply chains, particularly for intermediaries. Consumers can now order many items directly from a supplier's website, cutting out the intermediaries. Clothes, books and airline tickets are all increasingly purchased online, threatening the traditional business of high street shops and travel agents.

The 'make or buy' decision

Managing inputs is important for organisations of all types, as the cost of inputs can make up a significant proportion of the total cost of goods and services. As well as deciding how to manage the different aspects of the supply process, organisations must make a series of strategic decisions about the scope of their activities. In particular, they must decide which inputs they will obtain from other organisations and which they will produce or create themselves. This is usually referred to as the 'make or buy' decision, which must be made within the strategic context of the organisation.

Vertical integration

From an operations perspective, many organisations have found it desirable to perform as many activities in the supply chain as possible, from the supply of primary materials to delivery to the end customers, a policy known as **vertical integration** (from seeing the supply chain as having a 'top' and a 'bottom'). Vertical integration is attractive because it provides managers with the maximum amount of control over performance and cost. Perhaps the ultimate example of this was Ford's River Rouge car factory, opened near Detroit in 1920 to produce the Ford Model T. It was the most fully integrated manufacturing facility in the world, with raw materials being delivered to one end of the production process and a fully finished car driven out at the other. Ford went so far as to make its own iron and steel on the production site from the coal and iron ore delivered by massive freighters to giant warehouses. The plant even produced its own electricity and moved materials around on its own railway! Although this is a somewhat extreme example, up until the 1980s many Western firms pursued similar policies.

Outsourcing

A big drawback to vertical integration is that organisations are seldom capable of excelling equally at all the activities along their supply chain. From the 1980s onwards, there was a growing belief that organisations might improve their performances if they concentrated on the activities that they could perform particularly well: their 'core competencies', around which they should build a sustainable competitive advantage. They began to use outside suppliers to perform all other 'non-core' activities. This has led to a rise in **outsourcing**, the external purchase of goods and services that had previously been produced internally.

A good example of a non-core activity is advertising. Even very large organisations tend to use external advertising agencies. Other frequently outsourced activities include catering, information services, travel arrangements, security and cleaning. Even activities that have traditionally been considered to be 'core', such as aspects of human resource management (e.g., recruitment), IT management and even core marketing or research and development, have been outsourced in some organisations.

Recently, many organisations have moved dramatically away from the 'make' end of the make or buy spectrum towards the 'buy' end. Within the computer industry, for example, the trend since the invention of the PC has been towards assembling and away from designing and making the electronics and software. When PCs first appeared, major computer manufacturers, such as IBM, did everything from producing the silicon for chips to writing the operating software and programs, to maintaining the computers after they were sold. Today, most PCs are assembled almost entirely from purchased components, including the hardware (such as monitors, microprocessors and drives) and the software installed on the computer.

Another example that you might be familiar with is Benetton, the fashion clothing specialist. Benetton is expert at designing and retailing fashion clothing, which has a very short shelf life. To obtain the clothing for sale it relies on a network of textile firms and garment manufacturers which achieve quick turnaround and can react quickly to changing customer demand.

The virtual organisation

The term 'virtual organisation' describes an organisation that has outsourced the maximum conceivable level of activities. Such an organisation simply coordinates and directs the activities of other organisations, which perform all the transformations of materials and customers. The growth of virtual organisations has been facilitated by the internet because access to the physical facilities of the organisation, or the physical location of the organisation itself, is often irrelevant to the provision of services to customers or other businesses. Internet-based companies such as www. lastminute.com, which serves primarily as an intermediary between other service providers and consumers, need only have a minimal physical presence.

Virtual organisations are not confined to the internet. Nike, the well-known sports shoe company, can be thought of as a virtual manufacturer because it does not make any of its own products. It outsources all of its manufacturing operations, mostly to suppliers in developing countries where it can take advantage of low labour rates. Nike itself retains design and marketing of its products as its key in-house activities.

Managing relationships with suppliers and customers

Influence of Japanese practice

The research into Japanese manufacturing practices during the 1970s and 1980s not only brought such ideas as **total quality management** and JIT to Western attention, but also revealed that relationships between Japanese suppliers and customers were very different from those in North America and Europe (Womack et al., 1990). Western companies tended to view their suppliers as adversaries. Negotiations were seen as a kind of battle, in which victory could be achieved by squeezing ever more concessions from suppliers on cost, delivery or some other performance criterion, with little concern as to how this might affect the supplier's ability to achieve their promises or, in extreme cases, their very existence. Contracts for specific goods or services were placed on the basis of price and delivery. The threat of losing the business to a competitor was an ever-present incentive for suppliers to keep their prices 'sharp'.

In Japan, on the other hand, companies such as Toyota worked together with many of their suppliers to create long-term partnerships. The focus of the relationship was achieving mutually beneficial collaboration. By working together, the supplier and the purchaser could achieve genuine cost reductions, which the supplier could then reflect in the price charged to the purchaser. Cost reduction was not, however, the only objective. By working in collaboration, it was possible to improve the quality, flexibility, dependability and speed of supply to the purchaser. Many Western companies, by focusing on cost per unit as the primary objective, treated each contract with suppliers as an independent transaction. The best Japanese companies, in contrast, focused on building and sustaining relationships with suppliers. These close relationships were necessary in order to make JIT production systems work.

There is, however, a debate about the extent to which these principles are limited to particular industries (especially motor car manufacturing) or particular types of relationships between companies (typically an all-powerful purchaser and a smaller dependent supplier), or whether they can be applied more generally. The downside of such close relationships was experienced in 2000 by some UK clothing suppliers to the UK retail giant Marks and Spencer (M&S). In the face of fierce price competition, M&S rationalised its supplier base and moved the sourcing of much of its requirements to cheaper overseas suppliers. Over-reliance on M&S caused major financial problems for many UK suppliers (and was widely seen as a public relations disaster for M&S in the UK).

Reducing the supplier base

The term 'supplier base' refers to the number of suppliers with which an organisation deals.

For many years, most organisations in the West felt that it was sensible to maintain a large supplier base. It was believed that this would foster competition, enabling purchasers to play suppliers off against each other to achieve the lowest possible price. Also, multiple suppliers were maintained 'just in case' there was a problem with existing suppliers. In Japan, a different approach to supply base management developed: Japanese companies tended to have fewer suppliers than their Western counterparts and indeed, many Japanese companies dealt with only a single supplier for a part or component. In exchange for getting 100 per cent of the customer's business, the supplier was expected to be much more responsive to the customer's needs – particularly in reducing the amount of inventory held by the customer.

As part of the trend to follow Japanese practice, many Western organisations began to rationalise their supplier base. Of course, supplier rationalisation has its risks. It:

- increases the power of an individual supplier
- makes the customer vulnerable in case of supply disruptions, including natural disasters, strikes, transportation problems and fuel shortages.

As well as reducing the overall number of suppliers, organisations can rationalise their supplier base by reordering their relationships with suppliers. By rearranging them into a 'tiered' structure, as shown in Figure 2.14, an organisation can reduce the number of suppliers it deals with directly. This certainly simplifies its dealings with suppliers. Some suppliers move to the second (or even third) tier, even if the total number of suppliers does not increase. Volkswagen has used this strategy in its Brazilian car assembly plant, where cars are assembled from a number of distinct modules. Volkswagen purchases complete modules from a number of lead suppliers, each of whom is responsible for a particular module. Each lead supplier is responsible for dealing with all of the suppliers who provide inputs into that module.

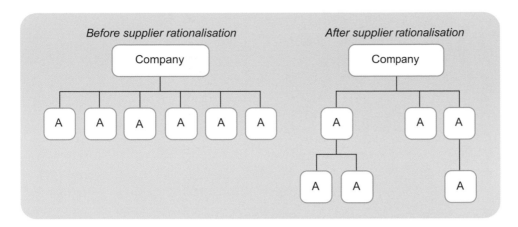

Figure 2.14: Before and after supplier rationalisation

Greater supplier involvement

Reducing the number of suppliers enables purchasers to devote much more time and effort to developing relationships with the remaining 'first-tier' suppliers. Increased supplier involvement is based on increased commitment by each party, which can create a partnership between buyer and supplier. If purchasers can identify their strategically important suppliers, they can involve them in planning for the future, enabling suppliers to invest and build their capabilities to meet future requirements. Similarly, instead of writing their own specifications for the goods and services that they need to purchase, they could work with their suppliers to develop the most appropriate specification, using the supplier's specialist expertise. Suppliers can also be involved in new product design and development. Purchasers can access their suppliers' in-house technologies and expertise, which can lead to more cost-effective and higher-quality designs.

Focusing on strategically important supply relationships

It should be obvious that an organisation cannot manage all supply relationships as if each were strategically important, especially if the organisation is applying strategic relationship management principles.

Stop and reflect

Given the large number of suppliers that even a simple organisation may deal with, how can managers decide which ones are strategically important for their organisation?

Kraljic (1983) developed a model that enables purchased products (whether goods or services) to be classified according to their strategic importance. Figure 2.15 shows the model as a two-by-two matrix. One dimension of the matrix shows how significant the cost of the input is to the organisation. The other dimension shows the risk to the organisation if the supply of the purchased product is interrupted. This is quite different from the cost of the product itself. Quite often, a seemingly insignificant item can have huge effects on an entire system.

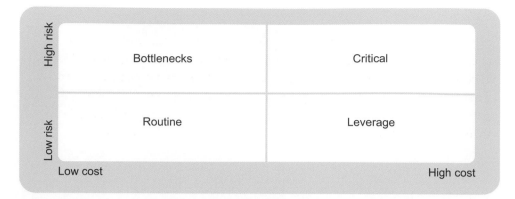

Figure 2.15: The strategic procurement matrix
(Source: adapted from Kraljic, 1983)

The strategic implications of the matrix are also important for managers. High-risk items, whether high cost or low cost, are strategically significant, while low-risk items of either sort are only tactically significant. The individual boxes are also each associated with a particular imperative:

- For *bottleneck* items, it is important to ensure that supplies are not interrupted.

- For *critical* items, the emphasis should be on cooperation with suppliers.

- For *routine* items, the imperative is to find the most efficient way to procure the product.

- Finally, for *leverage* items, it is important to find the best deal.

Establishing more strategic relationships between purchasers and suppliers requires honesty and commitment from both parties. In particular, trust within these relationships is beginning to be assessed from an operations viewpoint (although a considerable amount of research from a theoretical viewpoint, by economists, has recently appeared). The concept of trust is often illustrated by 'the prisoners' dilemma', with which you may be familiar.

The prisoners' dilemma

In this scenario, two people are accused of robbing a bank. However, a conviction can be achieved only if one or both confess to the crime. They are questioned separately by the police. Each is offered, unknown to the other, a lenient sentence for a confession that will implicate their partner. If one confesses, the other goes to jail for a long time. If both confess, they both go to jail for a shorter period. The best outcome for them is for neither to confess, as they will both then go free. However, this relies on each person trusting that the other will not confess.

Stop and reflect

How can two organisations build trust into their relationship?

Attempts to build trust between companies might include 'open book' relationships between supplier and customer, where the parties are given access to examine the other's financial accounts. It is particularly difficult for each partner to achieve trust when there are power differences between them. These might occur when one party has control over scarce resources (e.g., a patented technology or a unique input) or where one party is much larger than the other (a small supplier to a large customer or vice versa).

Conclusion to chapter 2

This chapter has addressed fundamental managerial theories, approaches and tools that are usually adopted in operations management practice.

Among the many important aspects covered in this chapter, we have seen that the design of processes should take into account the volume and the extent of variety required in the output of the operation. Different levels of volume and variety require different types of processes that will better deal with the production or delivery demand – that is, the process type for any good or service must be consistent with the volume and variety of the output. As volume increases it becomes difficult to customise output to individual customers. The choice of process type follows the strategic decision regarding the level of volume and variety an organisation wants to pursue and it will affect the design of the processes and the operations as a whole; different process types entail different arrangements in the layout and flow of the operations.

Many organisations have achieved high-volume and high-variety capability through using process technologies innovatively – that is, the equipment, machines, devices or systems that support the production and delivery of goods and services. Decisions about which process technology to adopt require careful consideration. More complex process technology decisions with long-term impact on the operations should take into account the impact of the technology on the operations ability to fulfil customer needs (market requirement evaluation), the additional capability and constraints the technology will bring to the operations (operations resource evaluation) and the financial value of investing in a specific process technology (financial evaluation). These three evaluation perspectives can be considered together with feasibility, acceptability and vulnerability aspects when assessing the technology.

Planning and control were other core operations aspects addressed in this chapter. While operations planning focuses upon the acquisition and management of the resources needed to support the production of goods or services in the future, operations control focuses upon the implementation of plans and adjustments necessary to make sure that the operations plan is achieved. Planning takes into account expected changes in technology and shifts in the demand for the organisation's goods or services. Control is concerned with meeting demand and utilising resources in the best way possible on a day-to-day basis.

Planning and control are essential management activities to help organisations to cope with demand fluctuations. Besides matching capacity and demand in the long term, organisations need to plan to make the best possible use of their existing capacity to meet demand in the medium and short terms. Levels of demand can be affected by short-term seasonal fluctuations, weekly fluctuations and daily fluctuations (peak and off-peak times). Some common strategies for matching capacity and demand are keeping the capacity constant despite demand fluctuations (level capacity), adjusting the capacity to meet the demand (chase demand) or changing the demand to match capacity (demand management).

Another important topic in this chapter was inventory management. Inventory generally refers to the stored accumulation (stock) of resources that are necessary in a specific transformation system (operation). In practice, all companies have some sort of resources stored as inventory, which is as important to service firms as it is to manufacturing organisations. Usually, service companies need to use materials in order to provide their services to the customers, and many services have physical products that form part of their outputs. Service companies can also use materials within their transformation processes, even if those materials are not part of the output supplied to customers. In essence, inventory exists to compensate for the differences in timing between supply and demand.

Chapter 2 finished with a section addressing the main aspects of supply chain management, which is another fundamental area of operations management. All operations, irrespective of their context and sector, have suppliers from whom they acquire their resource inputs and customers to whom they supply their outputs. Supply chain management activities encompass the acquisition, storage and movement of resources within an organisation and between the organisation and its environment. These activities are usually organised into main functional areas of supply chain management operations within organisations, namely purchasing, materials management, and physical distribution and logistics.

Logistics and supply chain management have a major impact on organisational performance figures. Supply chain decisions affect not only what goes on within the transformation process, but also the relationships with suppliers and customers. In general, logistics and supply chain management can reduce costs and add value for customers by providing customers with outputs that are right the first time and delivered quickly and punctually, at the lowest possible cost. It is about delivering the right product, at the right time, to the right customer and achieving this through the right means.

3: Improving operations

There are many reasons why improvement is an imperative for all organisations. No organisation, no matter how successful, can continue to thrive unless it improves its operations function's performance. For organisations that are not currently performing well, failure to improve their operations could threaten their survival. All organisations need to improve the outputs of their goods and services, and the processes that produce them, to ward off competition in all its guises. They must keep pace with the rising expectations of their customers, clients and other stakeholders. By improving the performance of their operations, organisations also develop the competencies and capabilities that will form the basis of their future strategies.

We have seen that operations managers are responsible for managing the processes that create and deliver an organisation's outputs of goods and services to customers. This requires their involvement in three important tasks: first, they need to contribute to designing those goods and services, and the processes that will produce them; second, they are responsible for the ongoing management of the organisation's operations. These are vital tasks but, even if they are performed satisfactorily, they would still leave the role of operations management incomplete, because the third task of operations managers, the one that is essential to all organisations, is to improve operations. This will be the focus of this chapter.

In this chapter, you will look at the main managerial philosophies and approaches that can be applied to improve the quality and performance of operations. You will also be able to understand how lean management principles and practices can be applied to improve operations.

Organisations' performance is continually challenged by the ever-changing nature of the external environment. This chapter will also develop your understanding of the major challenges that companies face when operating in a global context.

3.1: Deciding on what to improve

Improving operations presents many broad challenges. An initial challenge is to determine what to improve. It is unlikely that any organisation would be able to improve everything at the same time, even if this was desirable. Therefore, choosing what to improve is an important decision that operations managers are continually required to make. Improving operations performance also requires investments of time and other resources, which are in limited supply in all organisations. After deciding what to improve, operations managers must be able to set priorities for improvement.

In this section, we will consider different approaches to evaluating operational performance and how priorities for improvement can be determined. We will close the section by outlining a number of ways in which performance can be improved within the different contexts of manufacturing and service operations.

After studying this section, you should be able to:

- evaluate operations performance in order to identify improvement opportunities
- set priorities for operations improvement.

Assessing operations performance

A good place to start assessing what aspects of the operations function need to be improved is to consider how 'operations' contributes to the overall performance of an organisation. Many organisations have mission and vision statements; many others formally state their main organisational objectives. The way they propose to achieve those objectives is set out in the corporate strategy.

The operations strategy is the means by which the operations function contributes to the corporate strategy. The aims and objectives of the operations strategy must be congruent with the overall strategy of the organisation. Any set of corporate objectives implies consequent objectives for the operations function. These can be expressed in terms of the five operations performance objectives you read about in section 1.2: cost, quality, dependability, speed and flexibility. Wanting to know how the operation is doing means knowing which aspects of operations performance are most important. Different measures may be required to determine progress towards each of these objectives.

Performance measures, in themselves, are not particularly helpful in assessing performance. To be able to say whether the performance is acceptable requires some means of comparison, some kind of performance standard. There are four kinds of performance standards.

- Past performance – comparing current performance with past performance is quite common. Many organisations' management accounting systems include comparisons of this month's performance with the same period last year. Such performance standards have the advantage of being easy to determine, as the organisation will normally have the appropriate historical data. Also, improving on past performance is always desirable. Relying exclusively on such standards, however, can foster an inwardly focused culture which may ignore the demands of customers. Reducing last year's lead time of three months to two months this year may still leave many customers dissatisfied.
- Internal performance targets – these are internally generated targets based on some consideration of what seems fair and reasonable. Many organisations set their budgets on such a basis. While this can seem an attractive approach, there are often problems in determining what is 'fair and reasonable'. What is an undemanding target to one person may be an ambitious goal to another. This can lead to the worst kinds of political behaviour, characteristic of budgeting processes in many organisations. Internal performance targets can also reinforce an inward perspective, potentially ignoring customer requirements.
- Benchmark standards – these are standards derived from comparison with some external source. Benchmarks can be derived from the performance of a competitor or another organisation undertaking similar operations in

the same industry. This is termed 'competitive benchmarking'. An alternative approach is 'best practice benchmarking', where the performance of acknowledged exemplars in specific operations is taken as the standard. This often means looking outside your own industry to find the world leaders for that activity. **Benchmarking** can encourage an external perspective and a desire to learn from others. However, gaining access to comparative performance data can be problematic, particularly from commercial competitors. It can be similarly difficult to find out what practices are behind the performance figures. Choosing who to benchmark your organisation against can be critical. After all, you cannot achieve a competitive advantage merely by being as good as your competitors. A final criticism of benchmarking is that it may not involve any direct consideration of what customers require. Having all their suppliers performing equally badly will be of little use to customers.

- Absolute standards – these are standards taken to their limits, such as zero defects, zero lead time and zero inventory. Although these may not be achievable in practice, they can be used as the ideal against which actual performance is measured. Using absolute standards as working goals may be self-defeating, however – it can be very demotivating to know you have an unattainable target.

Setting priorities for improvement

Stop and reflect

How can managers prioritise the improvement of their operations?

Several of the ways of setting performance standards discussed above can be criticised for not explicitly taking the needs of customers into account. A fundamental tenet of marketing is that not all customers are the same and that markets can be segmented by identifying groups of customers with similar needs. From an operations point of view it can be helpful to understand the criteria that customers use when selecting between different goods and service offerings. Hill (2005) identified a distinction between **market-qualifying** and **order-winning** selection criteria.

- Market-qualifying criteria – are those characteristics of an operation's outputs that entitle it to be considered by a customer. For example, someone considering the purchase of an airline ticket for a flight next week will be interested only in those airlines that have a flight going to their desired destination for the day and time that they want to travel, and that tickets are still available. For this reason, market qualifiers are sometimes described as 'Yes/No' propositions. If an operation's performance falls below the qualifying level, it will not be considered as a potential supplier of a good or service. On the other hand, the amount by which it might exceed the qualifying level is irrelevant; it will make the user no more likely to choose the supplier.

- Order-winning criteria – are those characteristics of an operation's outputs that actually win orders in the marketplace. In the example above, the final decision about which airline to fly with might be based on the price of the ticket. Unlike with market qualifiers, the level of performance on order-winning performance objectives is important. Thus, improving performance in an order-winning criterion will increase the likelihood of the purchaser choosing the product.

In order to make their offerings most attractive to their chosen market segment, organisations need to make sure that they meet their customers' market qualifier and excel on their order winners. This distinction is illustrated in Figure 3.1, which shows the influence on acquirers of goods or services of improving operations performance in market-qualifying and order-winning criteria.

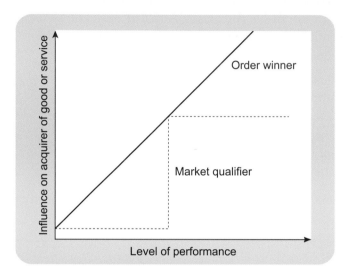

Figure 3.1: Market qualifiers and order winners

It is essential for an organisation to know how it is performing on the order winners and market qualifiers on which their potential customers base their selection and purchasing decisions. It can also be vital to realise that there may be groups of customers constituting distinctive market segments that have different order winners and market qualifiers. Furthermore, it is important to keep a constant watch on customer selection criteria, as order winners and market qualifiers may not be static, but may evolve over time, especially as the good or service passes from one phase of the product life cycle to another. The concept of order winners and market qualifiers can be used to help determine improvement priorities.

The performance-importance matrix

A useful tool to help with the analysis of operations performance is the **performance-importance matrix** (Slack et al., 2007) shown in Figure 3.2. The idea of the matrix is to provide a pictorial representation of how the operation performs against key performance criteria, and how much those criteria matter to the organisation's customers. To complete the matrix, managers consider each of the operation's performance criteria in turn. These are usually based on the five performance objectives of cost, quality, dependability, speed and flexibility. For each criterion the organisation's current performance is rated as 'worse than', 'the same as' or 'better than' the performance of key competitors. This gives that performance criterion a position on the vertical axis. Alternatively, current performance can be rated against that required by customers or against a selected benchmark standard. The position on the horizontal axis is given by rating the importance of each performance criterion (high, medium, low) to the operation's customers.

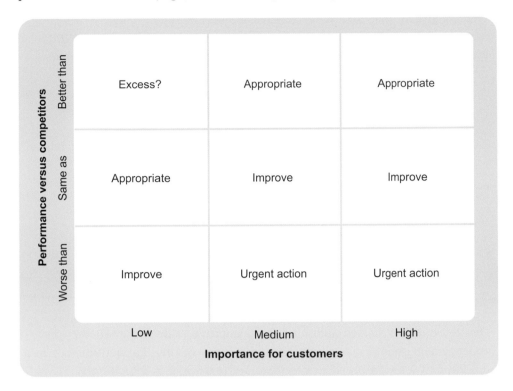

Figure 3.2: The performance-importance matrix
(Source: based on Slack et al., 2007)

The position of each performance criterion, once plotted on the matrix, helps managers decide on appropriate action for improvement, according to the advice given in each square. This is as follows, for each square.

- Appropriate – in these squares, performance is currently satisfactory. It is better than the competition in criteria that customers think are important, or as good as the competition in criteria that customers think are not important. However, it would be wise to monitor both ongoing performance to avoid becoming worse than the competition and customer preferences to ensure that any changes in their expectations are detected.

- Improve – in these squares, performance could be improved. However, it need not be given top priority, as it is the same as the competition in criteria that customers think are important and worse than the competition only in criteria that customers think are not important.

- Urgent action – these squares call for prompt action to achieve improvement. Here, the operations function's performance is significantly worse than competitors in criteria that customers consider as important.

- Excess – in this box, the operation's performance might be in excess of what is required. Performance is better than competitors, but in criteria that customers do not consider important. Consequently, valuable resources might be being consumed that could be better directed towards improving some other aspect of performance. For example, it is pointless achieving a delivery speed that is significantly better than the competition if customers place more value on the dependability of delivery.

3.2: How to improve operations

This section will explore the next step once an improvement opportunity has been identified; that is, how to achieve the improvement. Clearly, we cannot consider the detailed actions that might be required to improve any particular operation – that is beyond a general management book such as this. We shall, however, consider the underlying approaches to performance improvement that might be taken in relation to any operations process.

After studying this section, you should be able to:

- explain the advantages and disadvantages of both continuous and radical approaches to operations improvement
- characterise the TQM approach to improve business operations
- understand the main philosophy and principles underpinning 'lean management'
- explain how lean management practices can improve operations.

Continuous versus radical improvement

The key question in determining how to improve is deciding whether the improvement should take place through a series of ongoing activities or in a single giant leap. In broad terms, there are two ways in which an organisation can try to improve: **continuous improvement** (also known as incremental improvement) and radical improvement (also known as radical change). In continuous improvement, change takes place through a continuous series of small improvements. Radical improvement, on the other hand, seeks a significant one-off improvement. These two contrasting approaches are often claimed to be characteristic, respectively, of Japanese and Western (typically US) organisations and symptomatic of their differing underlying attitudes to management.

Continuous improvement

Continuous improvement is the relentless pursuit of improvements through a process of small, ongoing changes. The Japanese word *kaizen* (continuous improvement) is associated with bottom-up, people-driven continuous improvement. *Kaizen* is based on the belief that one should never be satisfied and should always seek to do better. Some of the techniques associated with *kaizen* include:

- quality circles: regular meetings of groups of workers to tackle quality problems and undertake improvement activities in their immediate work area
- employee suggestion schemes: encouraging, recognising and rewarding employees' suggestions for improving products and processes.

The continuous improvement approach is underpinned by a conviction that all employees have natural creativity that must be tapped into. It also acknowledges that the people who are closest to the organisation's operating processes – the operations staff – generally know more about processes than anyone else. Techniques such as quality circles and employee suggestion schemes can have an effect beyond simply the ideas that they produce because they can, if used effectively, foster a sense of ownership and involvement. They can energise those who work in the operations and help create the conditions that are essential for ongoing improvement: a sense of common purpose and agreed goals. Ideally, improvement becomes a natural part of everyday work.

Furthermore, the continuous improvement approach is reflected in the growing trend of empowering workers, increasing their level of responsibility and providing them with the resources necessary for solving problems in their work areas. The emphasis is less on controlling workers and more on gaining their commitment. This may also involve shifting the focus of responsibility from the individual to the team or group.

Continuous improvement is an essential feature of Japanese management techniques such as total quality management (TQM). In some respects TQM is *kaizen* applied to quality and its success is based on improvement being led from the bottom up, not imposed from the top down. They have now been widely mimicked in the West.

It is important to bear in mind that the success of Japanese manufacturing companies (motor cars, consumer electronics, etc.) in the 1970s and 1980s led many organisations, especially in the West, to copy Japanese practices in their operations. They adopted concepts such as TQM, JIT, **lean production**, agile manufacturing, mass customisation, world-class manufacturing, and so on that were promoted so enthusiastically by many academics and consultants. This whole approach is underpinned by the so-called 'best practice mentality', based on the idea that there is 'one best way' to manage operations (it is interesting to note that the scientific management approach of Frederick Taylor and others nearly a century ago was similarly derived from the belief that there is 'one best way' to perform any job or activity). Of course, each of the techniques borrowed from Japan has been used successfully by many organisations, but there are dangers and drawbacks in a 'one best way' approach to improving operations. The belief that there can be one solution for particular problems in all circumstances in all organisational contexts seems highly simplistic, if not misguided. And as some commentators have noted, it is impossible to achieve a competitive advantage merely by doing the same things in the same way as your competitors.

Radical improvement

Radical improvements are designed to provide a one-off, major advance in performance. Often they are associated with significant changes in design, operating processes and practices, and with big investments of money and other resources. They also rely on the introduction of new technology. It is claimed, with some justification, that managers in Western organisations have an over-reliance on radical improvement to achieve performance improvements. In particular, they tend to seek a technological 'fix' to achieve operations improvement. Hayes and Wheelwright (1984) contrasted this technological approach with the operations management approach (focusing on managing and improving the operations system as a whole) and the operations strategy (focusing on the long term by selecting a particular operations configuration to create a specific sustainable operational capability). It is easy to be seduced by the technological benefits alone, rather than assessing the business impact.

Radical improvement is likely to be effective when an organisation needs to completely change its performance to compete effectively, or even just to survive. Also, some operations are not amenable to gradual change and improvement may only be possible through radical solutions.

A typical example of a radical improvement initiative is **business process re-engineering** (BPR), which is a radical improvement approach based on the complete redesign of business processes. It usually involves the introduction of new working practices and new technology. BPR can be defined as:

> the fundamental rethinking and radical redesign of business processes to achieve dramatic improvements in critical, contemporary measures of performance, such as cost, quality, service and speed.
>
> (Source: Hammer and Champny, 1993)

BPR is based on the central tenet of operations management that processes are the key to understanding business performance. Thus, it takes a radical approach to performance improvement by re-examining business processes – that is, attempts to improve performance need to be based on a sound analysis of business processes, whether these processes transform materials, customers or information.

BPR shares a key idea with general operations improvement: while customers or clients purchase or use the outputs of operations, the processes that create and deliver these outputs are generally cross-functional rather than functional. In other words, the focus on improving operations needs to be cross-functional and process focused, rather than narrowly focusing on outputs. BPR advocates that organisations be structured around processes rather than the functions that have become the basis for most organisational structures, and that all business processes should be designed to add value from the customer's perspective, starting and ending with the customer.

Although its misuse and misrepresentation has given BPR a bad press (especially when large-scale job losses were involved), when used properly its techniques can provide a means for fundamental reassessment of business operations, which can lead to dramatic improvements in performance.

Stop and reflect

What are the main differences between continuous improvement and radical improvement? Think of an improvement initiative adopted in your company. Is it continuous or radical?

Radical improvement is often much more risky than continuous improvement, since it disrupts established ways of managing operations. It has also been argued that management often engages in such initiatives for more reasons than simply because they expect to achieve radical performance improvements. It is not too cynical to suggest that sometimes they have ulterior motives – they may wish to demonstrate to stakeholders that they are taking decisive action and that they are progressive (e.g., in using modern technology and management techniques). They may seek to weaken, or consolidate power over, groups of workers or gain power over rival management coalitions.

The differing impacts on performance over time of the continuous and radical improvement approaches are illustrated in Figure 3.3.

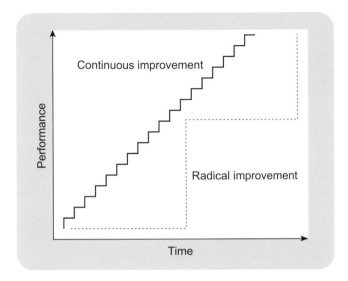

Figure 3.3: Continuous improvement versus radical improvement

As mentioned above, radical improvement is, by its very nature, risky – particularly the introduction of new and untested technology. Even if the technology can be made to work, it may not deliver the expected benefits. Most organisations have their favourite stories of new technology, often including IT failure. Major projects of this nature are inevitably difficult to manage. Change can be very threatening to many people and there can be the danger of 'initiative fatigue', as people are worn down by constant upheavals. If all change is large scale and radical, it can prompt a kind of short-term siege mentality – change is seen as something to be survived, before returning to normal life. This merely reinforces the perception of change as difficult and dangerous – something to be avoided rather than welcomed.

A final important point is that continuous improvement and radical improvement are entirely compatible. Many companies adopt both approaches in combination. An obvious advantage of continuous improvement is that it creates both a culture of change that permeates the organisation from bottom to top and a mindset in which people will embrace change. In this way, incremental improvement can be used as a foundation for more radical change, making it seem more natural and less traumatic. Similarly, there are advantages to be gained in adopting an incremental approach in order to seek continuous improvement after the introduction of new technology or some other radical change. Unless this is done, performance is likely to drop off as complacency slips in.

The total quality management (TQM) approach

In general terms, total quality management (TQM) is a philosophy of continuous organisational improvement. It places quality at the centre of all activities within an operation. The 'total' in TQM embraces every person in an organisation as well as everyone involved in the business as a whole, from suppliers to customers. TQM also focuses on the impact that every individual staff member of an organisation has on quality. It stresses the notion that each person in an organisation is responsible for getting quality right (Slack et al., 2007).

An important managerial concept that emerged from TQM is the concept of 'internal customer' and 'internal supplier'. This concept recognises that everyone within a company can be both a consumer of goods and services provided by other people within the same company as well as a supplier of goods and services to other people within the same company. From this perspective, the internal customer is any individual (or group of individuals) working in a transformation process that will transform the inputs provided by another individual (or group of individuals) working in other transformation processes within the company. Similarly, the internal supplier is any individual (or group of individuals) providing the outputs that will be transformed by another individual (or group of individuals) working in other transformation processes within the company.

This concept requires a clear understanding of the relationships between the processes within an organisation. In reality, all organisations comprise several processes that directly or indirectly contribute to the provision of the final good or service to the customers. The many processes of an organisation are internal transformation processes interacting (receiving inputs/feedback and/or providing outputs/feedback) with other internal transformation processes. Each smaller process contributes to part of the overall transformation process of the organisation, transforming or producing something that will contribute or add value to the overall transformation process that produces the final good or service. Figure 3.4 shows an expanded version of the transformation model, pointing out the internal processes or sub-processes of the main transformation process.

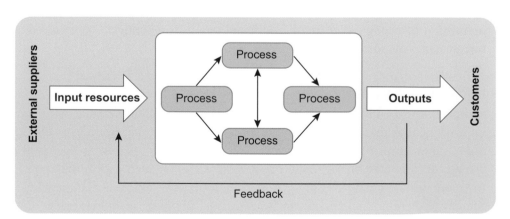

Figure 3.4: The transformation model expanded
(Source: adapted from Slack et al., 2007, p. 654)

The implication of the internal customer and internal supplier concept is that those involved in carrying out each 'supplier' process must clearly understand the requirements of their 'customer' processes so that the customers' needs and expectations can be fulfilled. A further implication is that every part of the organisation contributes to the satisfaction of the external customer by satisfying its internal customers. The ultimate purpose of the internal customer supplier concept is to create an internal chain of error-free services whose quality, speed, dependability, flexibility and cost-effectiveness will reach the external customer.

Stop and reflect

Is there any quality management initiative in your company that reminds you of the TQM approach?

Lean production

Lean production has its historical roots in Japan in the aftermath of the Second World War. At that time the country was struggling to re-establish its industrial base under conditions of great privation and severe shortages of resources of all kinds. Lean production also owes much to the unique character and context of Japan, a country with limited usable land and natural resources.

Lean practices took many years to emerge and are continuing to develop today. However, they are credited as being behind the undoubted success of the Japanese manufacturing industry in the latter half of the twentieth century. The managerial practices behind lean production were pioneered by Toyota in its innovative Toyota Production System, in which workers are organised in small teams or work groups. Each team is responsible for working on a particular phase of the production process and each team member is also responsible for continuously finding ways to increase quality and reduce costs and waiting times. An important innovation in the Toyota system was the development of the JIT concept, which is a 'pull'-based system in which inventory is moved ('pulled') downstream only when it is required by the next stage in the production. JIT allowed the elimination of **buffer inventories**, which are typical of traditional 'push'-based systems in which inventory is moved ('pushed') downstream according to a planned production forecast (Figure 3.5).

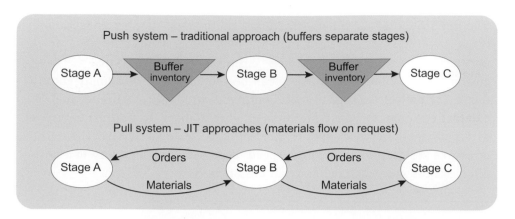

Figure 3.5: Push versus pull system
(Source: Slack et al., 2007, p. 467)

The 'lean' concept evolved in scope over time and today the term 'lean production' is widely adopted to refer to the philosophy of 'doing more with less' (i.e., less inventory, less space and fewer resources). Lean production has now become accepted wisdom and the basis of a so-called best practice or world-class model that its advocates argue should be adopted by all operations, services as well as manufacturing.

The lean approach to managing operations is based on three fundamental principles (Russell and Taylor, 2006):

- eliminating waste

- involving staff in the operation

- driving for continuous improvement of the operations function.

Eliminating waste concentrates on the elimination of all forms of waste, which, in general terms, is any activity that does not add value. Table 3.1 shows the seven types of waste that were identified by Toyota. These forms of waste have been found to apply to several different types of operations in both the manufacturing and the service sectors, and they are central to lean philosophy (Slack et al., 2007).

Table 3.1: The seven forms of waste

Overproduction	Producing more than is immediately needed by the next process in the operation Inventory ends up being held
Waiting time	Equipment efficiency and labour efficiency are two popular measures that are widely used to measure equipment and labour waiting time, respectively Less obvious is the amount of waiting time of items in a process needing to be further processed (work-in-progress inventory)
Transport	Moving items around the operation does not add value Layout changes bring processes closer together, improvement in transport methods and workplace organisation can all reduce waste
Process	The process itself can be a source of waste Some processes may exist only because of poor component design or poor maintenance and so could be eliminated

Inventory	Inventory should become a target for elimination
	However, it is only by tackling the causes of inventory that it can be reduced
Motion	An operator may look busy but sometimes no value is being added by the work
	Simplification of work is a rich source of reduction in the waste motion
Defectives	Quality waste is often very significant in operations
	Total costs of quality are much greater than has traditionally been considered and it is therefore more important to tackle the causes of such costs

(Source: Slack et al., 2007, p. 470)

Involvement of staff is about developing an organisational culture that encourages staff to take on much more responsibility, engagement and ownership of their job. Usual practices to increase the degree of personal responsibility and engagement include team-based problem solving, job rotation, multi-skilling, autonomy and quality of working life.

Finally, *continuous improvement* is an essential element of the lean philosophy. Continuous improvement was discussed earlier in Section 3.2.

Stop and reflect

Is your company adopting any of the main principles of the lean philosophy discussed above?

Improving manufacturing performance

Three important ways of improving manufacturing performance might be through factory focus, process flexibility and information technology. It is worth noting that although these initiatives were originally developed in a manufacturing context, they can also be applied to service organisations. They are described in more detail below.

Factory focus

A common problem with manufacturing operations is that they often evolve away from their original design, without proper consideration of how the various elements in the production evolve together. It has been argued that performance would be improved if each operations facility were to focus on a single task (Skinner, 1974). Where an organisation requires its manufacturing operations to perform multiple tasks, this could be done either by dividing operations between different facilities or by creating 'plants within a plant', in which each plant focuses on a single task.

This approach is based on the belief that every manufacturing operation needs to be configured to meet a specific market need. This requires managers to make a fundamental trade-off between different performance objectives, choosing one (e.g., low cost, fast throughput time, high flexibility) as its principal objective. This is in stark contrast to recent concepts of 'world-class manufacturing', which imply that an operation can excel on all performance criteria and need not configure itself for the achievement of a single primary objective.

Process flexibility

Since the original 'Fordist' (Henry Ford, car manufacturer) era of mass production in stable environments, the competitive challenges facing manufacturers in most markets have changed dramatically.

This creates the need for flexible operations. Flexibility is the ability of a process to change or react with little penalty in time, effort, cost or performance. Flexibility might involve changes in a set of tasks, in a set of customised products or across a broad product range. The dimensions in which a process may be expected to be flexible include:

- *volume* – the ability of the process to adjust to changes in the amount of output, whether higher or lower, without penalty.

- *product range* – the ability of the process to add to or take away from the number of outputs, without penalty

Flexibility is important because organisations often find themselves having to use their operations for purposes for which they were not originally designed, or have hitherto been used. These shifts in the demands on operations may be internal, perhaps brought on by product proliferation, or external, probably due to changing customer needs or wants.

A problem for many manufacturers and service providers that compete on low cost and standardised outputs is the inflexibility of their processes. For example, McDonald's fast-food hamburger restaurants are very good at producing variations in the elements surrounding the hamburger (e.g., special toppings), but less good at producing meals that are not cooked on a griddle.

A number of different terms are used to describe attempts to achieve flexible operations, including *agile production* and *mass customisation*.

Information technology

In the early 1980s, many operations management professionals predicted that, by the turn of the century, production would be taking place in fully automated factories. While we have not yet reached that stage, the use of information technology of all kinds, ranging from bar codes to robotics, has become commonplace in many operations processes.

An information system that has been widely deployed by many companies is the enterprise resource planning (ERP) system. ERP systems are designed to provide a fully integrated organisation-wide information system to control all activities, including purchasing, inventory, manufacturing, finance and personnel. While they can be expensive, it is claimed that they achieve major improvements in performance across the organisation.

However, there have been a number of notable failures, in among many successes, in implementing major IT projects. It is therefore wise to exercise some caution when seeking IT-based performance improvements. Major disappointment has often occurred when IT-driven change has been designed for implementation across the entire enterprise. A number of such projects have failed, and these failures have been widely publicised. For example, the public sector does not appear to have a higher failure rate in major IT projects than the private sector, but its failures tend to be much more highly publicised.

Improving service performance

In the service area, two important ways in which the performance of service delivery systems might be improved are increased customer involvement in the service process and increased use of customer feedback to improve service quality.

Increased customer involvement in the service process

The use of customers as part of the service delivery process is increasingly seen as a way of improving service operations' performance. It can be doubly beneficial, increasing both efficiency and customer satisfaction.

In many services, back-office operations (e.g., cheque-clearing in banks) are already run at extremely high levels of efficiency, largely thanks to manufacturing-based process improvement techniques. Most of the techniques that can be applied have already been implemented, and so it has become difficult to further significantly improve their performance. In the front office, however, there is a limit to how much work can be loaded on to those delivering the service to waiting customers. Consequently, the incorporation of customers in all or part of the service delivery process may offer the best chance of improving the efficiency of front-office operations.

Customers can become involved in various aspects of the service delivery process, as shown below.

- Specification – customers can become involved in designing the specification of the product, so that it can be customised to meet their particular needs and requirements (e.g., kitchen design).
- Co-production – customers can be used to perform some or all of the activities, such as serving themselves from a salad bar in a restaurant.
- Quality control – customers become responsible for the quality of part of the operation; for example, providing feedback or trying new developments.

Some organisations have been very successful at improving efficiency through increased customer involvement. At fast-food hamburger restaurants like McDonald's, customers perform most of the tasks that would be performed by employees in more traditional restaurants – notably, seating themselves, delivering food to their tables and clearing away rubbish at the end of the meal. Another successful organisation is IKEA, where customers collect their goods from the warehouse, deliver them to their own homes and assemble the furniture themselves.

A key to the success of such operations is that the customer can generally perceive the value of their contribution – for example, at McDonald's, by getting food more quickly and paying lower prices. This can create greater customer satisfaction. Some people have criticised increased customer involvement as involuntary unpaid labour. They see the growing 'McDonaldisation' of society, where customers provide a significant labour component of increasingly standardised services, leading to a situation where most services exploit their customers.

Increased use of customer feedback to improve service quality

Services differ from manufacturing operations in that perceptions of quality are often highly subjective and difficult to measure. Consequently, service providers need to rely much more on customer feedback to identify problem areas in which performance improvement actions should be initiated. Service operations need to understand quality from the customer's standpoint and to identify where operations do not meet customer expectations. Many tools from service marketing, such as the SERVQUAL gap model, can be applied by service operations management. Techniques for collecting customer feedback include self-completed customer questionnaires, face-to-face and telephone interviews, and customer focus groups. Improvement activities might range from the physical design of the service facility to the empowerment of employees and the split of activities between front and back offices.

3.3 Global challenges

Although operations managers are largely concerned with the routine aspects of their organisations, they constantly face major challenges imposed by the development of new technologies, ideas, environmental circumstances or business paradigms that potentially impact on their operations. For instance, the evolution of information and communications technologies associated with the development of more efficient global logistics systems has opened the doors for an increasing number of companies to operate worldwide. The consequence is that companies, whether or not they operate globally, are facing increased competition.

The fast-changing nature of the global business environment requires managers to respond in different and creative ways in order to maintain their competitiveness and improve their operations performance. It is therefore important for operations managers to understand the consequences of the global challenges they might face in order to adequately respond to them.

In this section, we will draw your attention to three topics of great magnitude that invariably bring significant challenges for the operations of organisations: **globalisation**, global logistics and **environmental responsibility**.

After studying this section, you should be able to:

- understand the nature of the global environment from a business perspective
- describe relevant operations and specific logistics practices in a global environment
- justify the importance of environmentally friendly operations initiatives.

Globalisation

The term 'globalisation' has been in use for many years. It can be described from different perspectives of the macro (or far) environment of organisations, addressing social, technological, economic, environmental and political dimensions. According to the International Monetary Fund (IMF), from an economic perspective the term 'globalisation' refers to 'the increasing integration of economies around the world, particularly through the movement of goods, services and capital across borders' (IMF, 2008, p. 2).

An important aspect of globalisation is that in order to harness the increased opportunities for international trade, many companies have developed overseas operations. In addition, it is no longer impossible for companies that do not have international operations – as is usually the case for small and medium-sized organisations – to sell and source products on a global dimension, as if the world were one large market.

Taking into account regional and local differences, many companies adopt a so-called 'glocalisation' strategy (think global, act local) when operating in a global context. The example below provides a good description of the term 'glocalisation'.

'Glocalisation' – think global, act local

One writer credited with bringing the term globalisation into mainstream use is the American academic Theodore Levitt. In a now famous 1983 article in the *Harvard Business Review*, Levitt suggested that companies must learn to operate as if the world were one large market – ignoring superficial regional and national differences. Much of what Levitt asserted in his article has stood the test of time and no doubt one can think of many global companies with global products. Conscious though of subtle yet often important regional and local differences, many companies now adopt a policy which some refer to as 'glocalisation' – thinking on a global world market scale, but adapting to local wants as appropriate. Just think, for example, of how McDonald's has both globally recognised and desired products (burgers, Coca-Cola, etc.) side-by-side with locally desired products in its many different restaurants across the world.

(Source: Mangan et al., 2008, p. 23)

Globalisation brings significant challenges for organisations producing goods and services with and for global partners. The cultural and economic particularities of different countries around the world do influence strategic and operational decisions concerning operations management.

Whether or not to develop international operations is a crucial decision concerning the international strategy of companies. This type of strategy is usually referred to as **offshoring**, the strategy of transferring specific operations to other countries with lower location costs. Usually, the lower costs are due to fewer regulatory controls and significantly lower wages (Mangan et al., 2008), which is why many people see globalisation as one of the causes of labour exploitation and corruption in developing countries. On the other hand, many others see it as a way of spreading prosperity to many people and companies throughout the world. According to Mangan et al. (2008), some of the reasons why companies decide to offshore include:

- lower location costs
- less stringent regulatory controls
- lower communication and IT costs
- improved capabilities of offshoring regions
- ability to cluster specific capabilities in certain regions.

Stop and reflect

What is the difference between offshoring and outsourcing?

It is important to realise that *offshoring* is not the same as *outsourcing*, where the ownership of the operations transferred to a provider company is also handed over to the provider. *Global outsourcing* is when the provider company is located abroad. In offshoring, the ownership of the specific operations functions transferred abroad remain with the company transferring them to the lower cost location.

At an operational level, some globalisation issues that should be taken into account by operations managers in their decision-making processes are listed in Table 3.2.

Table 3.2: Globalisation considerations for operations management decisions

Decision area	Some globalisation issues
Product/service design	Adaptation of design to fit culture and legislation (e.g., safety requirements)
Layout of facilities	Cultural reaction to work organisation (e.g., work conditions requirements)
Process technology	Maintenance of technology (e.g., maintenance costs) Skills availability in different regions
Capacity planning and control	Differences in seasonality and demand patterns Legislation for part-time and temporary work
Inventory planning and control	Storage conditions and climatic sensitivity Storage costs
Supply chain planning and control	Transport costs and infrastructure Supplier conformance to employment standards

TQM	Cultural view of acceptable quality
	Cultural view of participation in improvement groups

(Source: adapted from Slack et al., 2007, p. 681)

Global logistics

Logistics plays a crucial role in our globalised world. It is not only a key driver of globalisation and facilitator of international trade, but also a vital element for delivery of humanitarian and emergency aid. As Mangan et al. (2008) put it:

> The global economy today is increasingly interconnected with logistics playing an essential 'lubricating' role – just as oil lubricates a car engine (without oil the engine would quickly seize up), so too the global economy relies on efficient and effective logistics systems in order to function (just look for example what happens when transport services are delayed or there is industrial action at a port or airport).
>
> (Source: Mangan et al., 2008, p. 32)

Global sourcing

Global sourcing refers to the sourcing of goods and services from overseas countries. It involves identification, evaluation, negotiation and configuration of supply chains across multiple geographies (Slack et al., 2007). Global sourcing has been a major trend of supply chains in recent years. There are many factors promoting this trend. For example, the formation of free trade agreement blocs such as NAFTA (the North American Free Trade Agreement) and MERCOSUR ('*Mercado Común del Sur*', a free trade South American bloc) has made it easier to trade internationally.

More efficient transportation infrastructure systems, as well as more sophisticated cross-border operations, have also contributed to the development of global sourcing initiatives. However, one of the main reasons why companies decide to implement global sourcing operations is cost reduction. Considering that transforming and transformed resources and materials represent the largest costs of the operations of most companies, an obvious strategy to reduce costs is to source from wherever is cheaper (Slack et al., 2007). As the example below illustrates, many parts of the Barbie doll are sourced from different countries.

Barbie: the all-American girl

Conceived in 1959 as the all-American toy doll, Barbie today is a true global citizen! Originally made in Japan (and not in the USA), today different parts of Barbie are made in various different countries: for example her hair is still made in Japan, the plastic in her body comes from Taiwan, her cotton clothing from China, and the moulds and pigments used in production come from the USA.

(Source: Mangan et al., 2008, p. 23)

The main problems associated with global sourcing are the increased complexity of dealing with suppliers from different countries in the world, the risks of delays and 'hidden-costs' related to cross-border operations, such as material handling, inspection and storage processes, regulatory and documentation requirements, and transport and freight fees. Thus, the decision to adopt global sourcing alternatives should take into account all related costs as well as the potential risks and the performance of the services provided by third parties. Table 3.3 below highlights some key aspects that managers should consider when evaluating global sourcing opportunities (Slack et al., 2007).

Table 3.3: Relevant aspects of global sourcing alternatives

Aspect	Issues to consider
Purchase price	The total price, including transaction and other costs related to the actual good or service delivered
Transportation costs	Transportation and freight costs, including fuel surcharges and other costs of moving products or services from where they are produced to where they are required
Inventory carrying costs	Storage, handling, insurance, depreciation, obsolescence and other costs associated with maintaining inventories
Cross-border taxes, tariffs and duty costs	Sometimes called 'landed costs' – costs associated with customs duties, shipping, insurance and other related fees and taxes
Supply performance	The cost of late or out-of-specification deliveries, which, if not considered properly, can offset any price gains attained by shifting to an overseas source
Supply and operational risks	Geopolitical factors related to changes in a country's leadership, trade policy changes or instability caused by war or natural disasters – all of which may disrupt supply

(Source: Adapted from Slack et al., 2007, p. 411)

Humanitarian logistics

One of the most challenging areas for operations involving global logistics is the one related to **humanitarian logistics**. In general, humanitarian logistics is about ensuring that the resources necessary for alleviating the suffering of vulnerable people are transported, handled, stored and delivered in the most efficient and effective way possible. Depending on the circumstances of where and when the humanitarian aid is necessary, this can be a nearly impossible task. Large-scale, unpredicted disasters make the worst scenario for humanitarian logistics.

Humanitarian organisations usually have to operate against irregular demand patterns and unusual constraints, characterised by many disruptions and bottlenecks in the transportation, receipt, warehousing, tracking and delivery of relief resources. Logistical shortcomings and oversights in the humanitarian context may result in serious consequences for the victims of disasters, where the price of failure can be counted in lives. Therefore, humanitarian logistics is required to be both fast and agile, despite all difficulties involved in terms of planning operations without knowing when or where an event will take place, how many suppliers (organisations and individuals) will be involved or how many people will need relief.

Different from business logistics, humanitarian logistics usually deals with an undetermined set of suppliers and irregular demand during large-scale emergencies. The increased complexity of humanitarian logistics has much to gain from commercial logistics, and vice versa. Logistics play a crucial role in the provision of humanitarian aid, where people with the skills to identify priorities and coordinate transport, storage, handling and deliveries are vital in keeping the relief effort moving (Heaslip, 2008).

Environmental responsibility

Environmental responsibility has become an area of major concern for operations managers. Many issues in the area can be intimately connected to core operations management practices, such as designing production processes that do not consume large amounts of energy and analysing the environmental impact of products that cannot be recycled.

From an operations perspective, environmental responsibility is about achieving sustainability through the reduction of the environmental burden caused by the production of goods and delivery of services. For example, the way an organisation designs its products has significant implications for the recyclability of the goods produced. Similarly, process design impacts on the usage of energy and labour. Table 3.4 highlights some environmental issues that managers should consider when evaluating environmental aspects of operations.

Table 3.4: Environmental issues concerning operations

Operations aspect	Issues to consider
Product and process design	Recyclability of materials Waste generation Energy consumption
Layout of facilities	Energy efficiency Heating/refrigeration efficiency
Process technology	Waste and product disposal Noise pollution Fume and pollution emission Energy efficiency
Planning and control	Impact of extended operating hours Inventory obsolescence and wastage Packaging policy
Supply chain management	Efficiency of transport supply/distribution Transport pollution of frequent JIT supply
Quality	Scrap and wastage of materials Environmental impact of process failure

(Source: Slack et al., 2007, p. 686)

Stop and reflect

Why is it important for organisations to develop environmentally friendly operations?

Improving operations is largely centred on reducing waste and the use of energy. Taking this aspect into account, we can say that operations improvement is also about enhancing both the performance and the (environmental) sustainability of an organisation. The most important point to realise here is that reducing both waste and resources consumption not only saves cost for an organisation, but also improves its sustainability performance.

According to Porter and van der Linde (1995) environmental pollution is an indication of operations inefficiency, which reveals flaws in the design of the product or process. In their view, discharging pollution into the environment is a sign that operational resources have been used incompletely, inefficiently or ineffectively. Finally, they argue that there is no conflict between environmental responsibility and competitiveness: using resources productively is what makes for competitiveness today.

From an environmental perspective, sustainability is about using resources and materials derived from sustainable or renewable sources. Its main concern is pollution prevention rather than pollution control. More specifically, sustainability actually involves three major initiatives:

- Pollution prevention – preventing pollution from being created rather than cleaning it up after creation.

- Product stewardship – recognising that the environmental impact of a product goes well beyond the organisational boundaries of the company, including not only making the product, but also its sourcing, distribution, use and disposal. It involves designing products with low environmental impact by using recyclable parts and materials that have a low environmental impact themselves.

- Clean technology – investing in energy-efficient technologies that make better use of energy sources as well as renewable materials, reducing the use of natural resources and minimising (or eliminating) the level of pollution emission.

A more advanced initiative in the area of environmental responsibility is implementing the concept of *industrial symbiosis*, where organisations from the same or different sectors collaborate with each other to ensure that the waste or by-product generated by the operations of one organisation is used as input by another organisation. A typical example of the industrial symbiosis initiative is the eco-industrial park developed in the town of Kalundborg, Denmark, where different companies in the region collaborate to share resources and use each other's by-products. At the centre of this industrial park is a coal power plant which shares material and energy with the community and many other companies in the region. The surplus heat from the plant is used to heat thousands of local homes in the region, as well as a fish farm nearby. The sludge from the fish farm is sold as fertiliser. Other by-products from the power plant are sold as raw material for road building and the production of wallboard and cement by other manufacturers.

Stop and reflect

How do the global challenges discussed in this chapter relate to your company?

Conclusion to chapter 3

This aim of this chapter was to explore key managerial philosophies, approaches, concepts and models that can be applied to improve the quality and performance of organisations in operational terms. We have seen that failure to improve operations threatens a company's survival in the market, because customers and other important stakeholders naturally seek to develop their business with companies that perform well.

When managing operations improvement, an initial question that managers usually face is 'what should be improved?' In order to make this sort of decision, managers need to clearly specify crucial aspects of their operations whose performance will be continually monitored – that is, they need to establish key performance indicators that will be measured and checked on a regular basis. To be able to say whether the performance is acceptable, it is necessary to establish some references as well. These are usually based on past performance, internal performance targets, benchmark standards and absolute standards.

Managers must also be able to set priorities for improvement. A good starting point is to set priorities with their basis in customer needs, wants and preferences. This requires a good understanding of the criteria customers use when selecting between different goods and service offerings. A helpful framework for prioritisation is to specify which aspects of the operations' outputs are 'order winning' and which ones are 'market qualifying' in terms of customers' selection criteria. Order-winning criteria are those characteristics of an operation's outputs that actually win orders in the marketplace, whereas market-qualifying criteria are the ones entitled to be considered by the customers.

Another crucial aspect of operations improvement is establishing how to achieve improvement. Two overall approaches to improvement were discussed in this chapter: continuous and radical. While the continuous approach focuses on ongoing small changes, the radical approach is more about a step change designed to provide a one-off major improvement in performance.

Total quality management (TQM) and 'lean production' were also discussed. TQM is a major management initiative based on a continuous improvement approach. It places quality at the centre of all activities within an operation, and the 'total' in TQM embraces every person in an organisation as well as everyone involved in the business as a whole, including customers and suppliers. The 'lean' concept evolved in scope over time; today, 'lean production' is widely adopted to refer to the philosophy of 'doing more with less' (less inventory, less space and fewer resources). Lean production has now become accepted wisdom and the basis of a so-called best practice or world-class model. It is based on three fundamental principles:

- eliminating waste

- involving staff in the operation

- driving for continuous improvement of the operations function.

The final section of chapter 3 focused upon global aspects of the business environment. The concept of 'offshoring', the strategy of transferring specific operations to other countries with lower location costs, was introduced. The ownership of the specific operations transferred abroad in offshoring remains with the company transferring the operations; this differs from 'outsourcing', where the ownership of the operations transferred to a provider company is also handed over to the provider.

After discussing global sourcing and the challenges inherent within humanitarian logistics initiatives, we turned our attention to the growing importance of the environmental responsibility of organisations. We saw that, from an operations perspective, environmental responsibility is about achieving sustainability through reducing the environmental burden caused by the production of goods and delivery of services. An important point to realise is that reducing both waste and resources consumption not only saves cost for an organisation, but also improves its business and environmental sustainability performance.

Conclusion to the book

This book has provided you with a good overview of the main concepts, practices, perspectives, approaches, tools and philosophies involved in managing operations. It took you on a brief journey through the operations world, starting with a comprehensive characterisation of the operations function and operations managers; going through the discussion of core operations management practices; and finishing with a presentation of key managerial approaches applied to improving the performance of operations and discussing some contemporary issues challenging organisations in our globalised world.

We hope that, after reading this book, you have come to realise that every manager somehow faces organisational situations that can be better dealt with by operations management practices, from the execution of simple tasks to the implementation of more complex processes involving several departments and people. We hope that you have also realised that a good understanding of the principles of operations management is important for all managers, because it provides a pragmatic way of understanding and managing organisations.

Finally, we hope that you make the most of your learning experience with this book by applying course concepts and frameworks to the workplaces and organisations in which you work.

Glossary

Batch processes

Processes of a batch production system. Batch processing is based on the processing of batches of products together, but each batch has its own process route and outcome.

Benchmarking

Comparison of methods and other aspects of processes, with the purpose of learning from them and assesing performance.

Buffer inventory

Inventory stocked with the purpose of compensating for unexpected fluctuations in supply and demand. It can also be called safety inventory.

Business process re-engineering (BPR)

A radical improvement approach based on the redesign of processes to fulfil external customer needs.

Business strategy

The main strategic positioning of a business unit in relation to its customers, markets and competitors. It is a subset of corporate strategy.

Capacity

The maximum level of value-added activity that an operation or process is capable of over a certain period.

Chase demand

A capacity management approach that adjusts output and/or capacity according to fluctuations in demand.

Continuous improvement

An improvement approach that assumes many, and relatively small, incremental improvements in the operations performance. It is also known by the Japanese term *kaizen*, and it contrasts with radical or breakthrough improvement.

Continuous processes

Processes of a continuous production operation, where the system is highly automated and runs with only intermittent stops (sometimes an endless flow). Typical of high-volume and low-variety production.

Control

The process of monitoring operations activity in order to allow for adjustments and coping with any deviations from the plan.

Cost

A crucial operations performance factor related to the economic efficiency of an organisation's operations. The cost effectiveness is important to all parts of the operations function.

Customer-processing technologies

Customer-driven technologies. They are technologies operated directly by the customers or by intermediaries.

Demand management

A capacity management approach that attempts to change or influence demand to fit available capacity.

Dependability

A critical operations performance factor. It is about delivering, or making available, goods or services as promised to the customer.

Dependent demand

Demand which is relatively predictable because it is derived from other known factors.

Direct process technology

Technology that contributes directly to the production and delivery of final goods and services.

E-business

Business processes or models that are totally based on or supported by internet-based technologies.

E-commerce

Internet-based operations and business processes that involve buying and selling activities. It can be seen as a subset of a wider e-business model.

Environmental responsibility

Activities and decisions in operations management that aim at minimising the negative impact of processes, goods and services on the environment.

EPOS

Electronic Point of Sale. An electronic device that registers and processes customers' purchases.

Flexibility

A critical operations performance factor. It is the degree to which an operation's process can change both how and what it does.

Flexible manufacturing system (FMS)

A manufacturing system in which separate machines or devices are under the control of a central computer, which coordinates the operations and finds the best timetables for specific tasks.

Flow

Important element of process design. It refers to how materials, information, or customers move through the operations system.

Forecasting demand

The estimation of future demand for goods or services delivered by an organisation.

Global sourcing

The sourcing of goods and services from other countries.

Globalisation

The extension of operations activities to cover the whole world.

Humanitarian logistics

Logistics operations aimed at ensuring that the resources necessary for alleviating the suffering of vulnerable people are transported, handled, stored and delivered in the most efficient and effective way possible.

Independent demand

Demand that is not directly dependent on the demand for another good or service.

Indirect process technology

Technology that is peripheral to the actual creation of goods and services, assisting in the management of processes rather than contributing directly to the creation of goods and services.

Information-processing technology

Generally known as information technology (IT). Any computer-based device or system that collects, processes, stores or distributes information.

Internal customers

Processes or individuals within an operation that can be seen as customers for other internal processes or other individuals' outputs within the operation.

Internal suppliers

Processes or individuals within an operation that can be seen as suppliers of products or services to other processes or individuals within the operation.

Inventory

Also known as stock. It is the accumulated storage of transformed resources in an operation. It typically refers to tangible materials but can also refer to inventory of intangible resources such as information.

Jobbing

Processes that deal with many different jobs according to specific customer requirements. Work is intermittent, rather than continuous. Each customer job is processed by the operation individually and may experience many different work activities before work is complete.

Just-in-time (JIT)

A method of operations planning and control based on the pull scheduling philosophy, in which, if the next process in a production or service delivery system is not ready to receive any inputs, the previous process will not produce any, thus minimising the amount of just-in-case or wasted stock.

Kaizen

Japanese term for continuous improvement.

Layout

Important element of process design. It refers to the arrangement of physical facilities for producing goods and services.

Lead time

The period of time between order and delivery of a good or service.

Lean production

A production approach based on the philosophy of 'doing more with less' (less inventory, less space and fewer resources).

Level capacity strategy

A capacity management approach that keeps the output from an operation or its capacity constant, irrespective of demand.

Logistics

An extension of physical distribution management, including all the processes involved in physical distribution, both into (inbound logistics) and from (outbound logistics) the organisation.

Make-to-order

Operations that produce products only when they are ordered by the customer.

Make-to-stock

Operations that produce products for stocking, prior to their being ordered by the customer.

Market-qualifying competitive factors

The characteristics of an operation's output that entitle it to be considered by a customer.

Mass production processes

Processes based on the production of large volumes of standardised products targeted to a mass market. A production approach appropriate for markets that demand high volumes of a similar output.

Materials-processing technologies

Technologies that process one or more types of material, such as chemicals, fabric, metals, plastics, etc.

Offshoring

Transference of specific operations to other countries with lower location costs. The ownership of the specific operations transferred abroad remains with the company transferring the operations.

Operations function

The arrangement of resources that are necessary to the production and delivery of goods and services.

Operations management

The activities and decisions related to the management of the production and delivery of goods and services.

Operations managers

The members of staff of an organisation who are responsible for managing some or all of the resources that constitute the operation's function.

Order-winning competitive factors

The characteristics of an operation's output that actually win orders in the marketplace.

Outsourcing

Transference of specific operations to another company, which will be the supplier of the work previously done by the company contracting the operations.

Performance-importance matrix

A useful tool that combines scores that indicate the relative importance and relative performance of different competitive factors in order to prioritise them for improvement.

Physical distribution management

Activities related to the management of the movement of goods and services to customers.

Planning

In operations, planning is concerned mainly with the definition of the adequate levels of resources necessary to the transformation process to create outputs, taking account of expected changes in technology and shifts in the demand for the organisation's goods or services.

Process

A linked chain of tasks or activities necessary for the fulfilment of customer requests. It usually cuts across different departments and functional units of an organisation.

Process technologies

The machines and devices used in the production of goods and delivery of services to customers.

Project processes

Processes related to an operations system that typically produces one finished output at a time to customer requirements. They usually deal with discrete and highly customised products.

Pull system

An operations production system in which a workstation requests work (inputs) from the previous station only when it is required. This system model is one of the fundamental principles of just-in-time.

Purchasing

A specific department or sector of the operations function that is responsible for acquiring transformed and transforming inputs from suppliers.

Push system

An operations production system in which a workstation sends forward inputs to other workstations as soon as it is finishes the production work.

Quality

A critical operations performance factor. It is about the consistent production of goods and services according to customers' expectations.

Resource-to-order

The operation only acquires resources for the production of goods or delivery of services when it receives a customer order.

Scheduling

A planning and control activity concerned with matching the flow of inputs and outputs on a short-term, often day-to-day, basis.

Sequencing

A planning and control activity concerned with assigning priority to tasks, deciding on the order in which work is to be performed.

Speed

A critical operations performance factor. It is about delivering goods and services to customers as fast as possible. It involves making quick decisions and rapidly moving materials and information inside the operations.

Stakeholders

The people or groups of people who have an interest in the operation and who may be influenced by, or influence, the operation's activities.

Standardisation

The extent to which processes, goods and services are prevented from varying over time.

Supply chain

A chain of operations that provides goods and services necessary for the fulfilment of end customers' orders.

Total quality management (TQM)

A holistic improvement approach to the management of quality. It emphasises the role of all parts and people within an organisation to influence and improve quality.

Transformation model

A diagrammatic overview of the main inputs, transformation processes, outputs and feedback mechanisms of an operation. It provides a systems perspective of the operations.

Transformed resources

The inputs of a transformation process that are transformed into outputs of the operations. Usually, they are a mixture of materials, information and customers.

Transforming resources

The resources of a transformation process that act upon the transformed resources. They comprise the facilities and staff in the production or delivery process.

Variety

The range of different outputs (products and services) produced by a process.

Vertical integration

The extent to which an operation chooses to perform the activities in the supply chain, from the supply of primary materials to delivery to end customers. It is often associated with 'make or buy' decisions.

Volume

The amount or level of output from a process.

References

Brown, S., Blackmon, K., Cousins, P. and Maylor, H. (2001) *Operations Management: Policy, Practice and Performance Improvement*, Oxford, Butterworth-Heinemann.

Chase, R. and Hayes, R. (1991) 'Beefing up service firms', *Sloan Management Review*, Autumn, vol. 33, no. 1, pp. 33-39.

Galloway, L., Rowbotham, F. and Azhashemi, M. (2000) *Operations Management in Context*, Oxford, Butterworth and Heinemann.

Hammer, M. (1996) *Beyond Reengineering*, London, HarperCollins Business.

Hammer, M. and Champny, J. (1993) *Re-engineering the Corporation*, London, Nicholas Brealey.

Harrison, M. (1996) *Principles of Operations Management*, London, Pitman Publishing.

Hayes, R. and Wheelwright, S. (1984) *Restoring our Competitive Edge: Competing through Manufacturing*, John Wiley & Sons.

Heaslip, G. (2008) 'Humanitarian aid supply chains' in Mangan, J., Lalwani, C. and Butcher, T. *Global Logistics and Supply Chain Management*, Chichester, John Wiley & Sons.

Hill, T. (2005) *Operations Management*, second edition, Basingstoke, Palgrave Macmillan.

International Monetary Fund (2008) 'Globalization: A brief overview', *Issues Brief*, iss. May, 02/08.

Kraljic, P. (1983) 'Purchasing must become supply management', *Harvard Business Review*, vol. 61, no. 5, pp. 109–17.

Levitt, T. (1983) 'The globalization of markets', *Harvard Business Review*, May–June, vol. 61, pp. 92–102.

Mangan, J., Lalwani, C. and Butcher, T. (2008) *Global Logistics and Supply Chain Management*, Chichester, John Wiley & Sons.

Neely, A. (1998) *Measuring Business Performance*, British Books for Managers (BBM), London, The Economist Books.

Pine, B. (1992) *Mass Customization*, Harvard, Harvard Business School Press.

Porter, M. (1985) *Competitive Advantage*, New York, The Free Press.

Porter, M. and van der Linde, C. (1995) 'Green and competitive: ending the stalemate', *Harvard Business Review*, September–October, vol. 73, pp. 120–134.

Reck, R. and Long, B. (1988) 'Purchasing: a competitive weapon', *International Journal of Purchasing and Materials Management*, Fall, vol. 24, pp. 2–8.

Russell, R. and Taylor, B. (2006) *Operations Management: Quality and Competitiveness in a Global Environment*, fifth edition, Hoboken-NJ, John Wiley & Sons.

Schmenner, R. (1986) 'How can service businesses survive and prosper?', *Sloan Management Review*, vol. 27, no. 3, pp. 3–29.

Skinner, W. (1974) 'The focused factory', *Harvard Business Review*, May–June, vol. 52, pp. 113–21.

Slack, N., Chambers, S. and Johnston, R. (2007) *Operations Management*, fifth edition, Harlow, FT Prentice Hall.

Slack, N. and Lewis, M. (2002) *Operations Strategy*, Harlow, FT Prentice Hall.

Waters, D. (2002) *Operations Management: Producing Goods and Services*, second edition, Harlow, FT Prentice Hall.

Womack, J., Jones, D. and Roos, D. (1990) *The Machine that Changed the World*, New York, Macmillan.

Acknowledgements

Grateful acknowledgement is made to the following sources.

Tables

Tables 3.1, 3.2, 3.3 and 3.4: Adapted from Slack, N., Chambers, S., & Johnston, R. (2007). *Operations Management*, Fifth edition, 2007 (Pitman Publishing), Pearson Education;

Figures

Figure 1.1: Porter, M. (1985) *Competitive Advantage – Creating and Sustaining Superior Performance*, The Free Press;

Figure 1.2: Galloway, L., Rowbotham, F., and Azhashemi, M., The transformation process, The context of operations management, *Operations management in context*, Elsevier Butterworth-Heinemann;

Figure 1.4: Neely, A (1998) *Measuring Business Performance*, British Books for Managers. Cambridge University Press;

Figure 1.5: Slack, N., Chambers, S., & Johnston, R., *The five key strategic performance objectives*, www.pearson.co.uk;

Figures 2.8, 3.4 and 3.5: Slack, N., Chambers, S., & Johnston, R. (2007) *Operations Management*, Fifth edition, 2007 (Pitman Publishing), Pearson Education;

Figure 2.13: Reck, R.F. and Long, B.G. (1988) A four stage model of purchase, Purchasing; a competitive weapon, *International Journal of Purchasing and Materials Management*, National Association of Purchasing Management;

Figure 2.15: Kraljic, P. (1983) 'Purchasing must become supply management', *Harvard Business Review*, vol. 61, No. 5, pp. 109–17;

Figure 3.2: Slack, N. (1994) 'The performance-importance matrix as a determinant of improvement priorities', *International Journal of Operations and Production Management*, 14(5), pp. 59–75, MCB University.